THE BEST OF ROME IN 6 WALKS

WALK 1 : … AZZA NAVONA …

This is one … through the … and admire the old streets.

WALK 2 > COLOSSEUM & MONTI p. 38

Marvel at the eternal Colosseum, visit the Forum and Palatino, then linger over an aperitivo in Monti.

WALK 3 > PANTHEON, GHETTO & AVENTINO p. 58

Walk south through the Ghetto and across the Aventino. Toward the end, you'll find unforgettable views from Giardino degli Aranci.

WALK 4 > VATICANO, BORGO & PRATI p. 78

Vatican City might be a small country, but it has the largest, most overwhelming art collection in the world. Recuperate with lunch in the Borgo and go shopping in Prati.

WALK 5 > REPUBBLICA, TRIDENTE & VILLA BORGHESE p. 98

Lush fountains, impressive palazzos, and stately obelisks. Stroll the exclusive Via Margutta and wander through the green Villa Borghese to see Bernini's finest sculptures.

WALK 6 > OSTIENSE, TESTACCIO & TRASTEVERE p. 118

The industrial district Ostiense is the southern end of this route. Beyond Testaccio, you get to Trastevere—which translates to "the other side of the Tiber"—and a great view of the city.

LA PIZZA
DEL TEATRO
APERIPIZZA
DEGUSTAZIONE DI
3 TIPI DI PIZZA E
BIRRA INCLUSA!
SPECIAL PRICE €10
DALLE ORE 17.30
ALLE 20.00
FARINE MACINATE A PIETRA 100% BIO
BIRRA ARTIGIANALE ALTA E
FERMENTAZIONE SUPPLI

LOCAL
MAUD NOLTE

CITY
ROME

WORK & ACTIVITIES
MARKETING

Maud emigrated to Rome in December 2020 due to her husband's work. Her favorite pastime is exploring the city and finding the newest gems. Her Google Maps app is filled to the brim with tips and a to-do list for friends, family, and now also for our readers!

MOON ROME WALKS

Step off the plane and head straight for the hippest neighborhoods. Find out where you get the best fish or pasta in the city and where to find locally brewed beer on tap. In *Moon Rome Walks* you'll find inside information on numerous hidden gems. This way, you can skip the busy shopping streets and stroll through the city at your own pace, taking in a local attraction on your way to the latest and greatest concept stores, as well as neighborhood parks where Romans hang out. Savor every second and make your city trip a truly great experience.

ROME-BOUND!

You're about to discover Rome! According to legend, Rome was built in 753 BCE, yet almost 2,800 years later the city is still very contemporary. The six walks will take you past all the Roman highlights, from the Campo de' Fiori to the Colosseum and from Piazza Barberini to the Trevi Fountain and the Spanish Steps. You can see twenty-eight centuries pass you by, where medieval neighborhoods sprung from ancient remains and where Renaissance palazzos and then Baroque churches were built. Nineteenth-century working-class neighborhoods are given a second life with murals, hip stores, and wonderful restaurants. But the espresso bar remains the espresso bar and tradition is never far away.

ABOUT THIS BOOK

In this book, our local author shares with you the genuine highlights of the city she loves. Discover the city on foot and at your own pace, so you can relax and experience the local lifestyle without having to do much preparation beforehand. That means more time for you. Our walks take you past our favorite restaurants, cafés, museums, galleries, shops, and other notable attractions—places we ourselves like to go. So who knows, you might even run into us.

None of the places mentioned here has paid to appear in either the text or the photographs, and all text has been written by an independent editorial staff.

PRACTICAL INFORMATION

The six walks in this book allow you to discover the best neighborhoods in the city. They will take you past museums and notable attractions, but more importantly they'll show you where to go for good food, drinks, shopping, entertainment, and an overall good time. Check out the map at the front of this book to see which areas of the city the routes will take you through.

Each walk is clearly indicated on a detailed map at the beginning of the relevant chapter. The map also specifies where each place mentioned is located. The color of the number lets you know what type of venue it is (see the key at the bottom of this page). A description of each place is then given later in the chapter.

LEGEND

- >> SIGHTS & ATTRACTIONS
- >> FOOD & DRINK
- >> WALK HIGHLIGHT
- >> SHOPPING
- >> MORE TO EXPLORE

Without taking into consideration extended stops at any one location, each route will take a maximum of three hours. The approximate distance is indicated at the top of the page before the directions.

Tip: As you walk through the city, it's easy to focus on just getting from one historical monument to the next, but remember to stop occasionally to look up and absorb your surroundings. It's a beautiful city!

PRICES

Next to the address and contact details of some listings, we give an idea of what you can expect to spend there. For sights and attractions, we indicate the cost of a regular, full-price adult ticket. For restaurants, unless otherwise stated, the amount given is the average price of a main course.

WHEN IN ROME

Your idea of efficiency will probably be challenged when visiting Rome. So relax and don't worry too much when you can't find an up-to-date timetable. There

may be a restaurant that opens later than its sign says or a museum that closes sooner than listed.

Most stores close for lunch—roughly between 1:30pm and 3pm—and are closed Monday mornings and all day on Sundays.

If you want to visit churches, keep a modest dress code in mind. Bring a light scarf to cover your shoulders on warm summer days, and make sure bare legs are covered. Skirts or shorts that fall below the knees are usually okay.

Since July 2014, museums in Italy have had a new policy. While a museum ticket used to be free for seniors sixty-five and older, now they must pay full price. To compensate, museum nights are organized twice a year. Major attractions like the Colosseum remain open until 10pm every Friday. And all museums are free the first Sunday of every month. Are you under eighteen or a student under twenty-six? Take your passport or student ID with you when you visit a museum. You'll get a discount, but only with identification.

EAT LIKE THE ROMANS DO

Eating is a vital part of Italian life. Romans tend to eat a late dinner, and only the most touristy restaurants open their doors before 7:30pm. Lunch is usually from 1pm to 3pm. Avoid restaurants where waiters stand outside praising the menu. Instead, it's hard to go wrong by choosing a Roman trattoria or osteria. The bill might include an amount for "coperto" or "pane"—a cover charge of about two or three euros per person. Unlike in the US, tipping is not customary, but you can leave one if the service is exceptionally good.

Typical Roman dishes include pasta carbonara, cacio e pepe, amatriciana, and artichokes. Be sure to try the traditional Roman supplì (a rice ball filled with cheese) and la cicoria (chicory), perhaps the most Roman of all foods (just order a portion—you'll be glad you did).

Romans don't eat an elaborate breakfast. They usually have a cappuccino and a cornetto (croissant) at their neighborhood bar. Pay at the checkout first, then take your receipt to the bar to collect your order. You're in and out in a matter of minutes. You can be served at a table, but you will be charged slightly more.

Aperitivo is the moment of the day dedicated to relaxation: settle down with a drink and a few nibbles after a busy afternoon or before dinner.

PUBLIC HOLIDAYS

August is the main holiday month for the whole of Italy. Many shops and restaurants will be closed in Rome for vacation (chiuso per ferie). Although this guide doesn't specify months in the opening hours of each listed place, please keep the month of August in mind when planning your trip. In addition to New Year's Day, Easter, and Christmas, Italy observes the following public holidays:

January 6 > Epiphany (La Befana)
April 25 > Liberation Day
May 1 > Labor Day
June 2 > Celebration of the Republic (Festa della Repubblica)
August 15 > Assumption of Mary (Ferragosto)
November 1 > All Saints' Day
December 8 > Immaculate Conception
December 26 > Boxing Day/St. Stephen's Day (Santo Stefano)

TRANSPORTATION

A taxi from Leonardo da Vinci Airport (Fiumicino) to the historic city center (within the Aurelian walls) costs €50, and from Ciampino Airport it's €30. At both airports, there may be unofficial taxi drivers who scam tourists. So, look for the official taxi queue and be sure to get into a white car with a taxi meter. You can also take the shuttle bus (www.sitbusshuttle.it, www.terravision.eu) to Termini station in central Rome. One way on the Leonardo Express train from Fiumicino to Termini costs €14, and to Trastevere station is €8. Rome's center is not very big, so you can easily explore on foot.

Caffé Doria
Caffè Doria
Caffè Doria
59

PUBLIC TRANSPORT

Rome has three subway lines. A and B cross each other at Termini station and pass by most of the major sites. Lines A and C cross at San Giovanni. Normally the subway runs from 5:30am to 11:30pm (Fri & Sat until 1:30am). The bus takes you to all the places the subway doesn't go, but buses are often late and jam-packed, and they are a favorite spot for pickpockets. Tickets for the subway, bus, tram, and train are €1.50 and are valid for one hundred minutes. On the bus, you must stamp your ticket at the yellow device when you get on. Please note, you can use one ticket to transfer between subway lines on the same trip, but you must stay within fare gates. Tickets are sold at tobacco shops (tabacchi) and subway stations. You can choose from one-day tickets (€7), two-day tickets (€12.50), three-day tickets (€18), and one-week tickets (€24). Night buses run between midnight and 5am. For more information, check out www.atac.roma.it.

A three-day Roma Pass (www.romapass.it) gives you unlimited access to public transportation; it also gives you free admission to two museums. It costs €52, and you can buy it at several tourist information points, all participating museums, and a few subway stations.

TAXIS

Taxis are not allowed to stop on the street and can pick up customers only at a taxi stop. Make sure your driver turns on the meter. If you have luggage, you pay extra, and prices are higher after 10pm and on Sundays and national holidays—starting at €5. You do not have to tip, and you can order a taxi by calling 06-3570.

SCOOTERS

If you're adventurous, rent a motor scooter (about €40 per day). You need a driver's license, and you must wear a helmet. Go to Treno e Scooter (rent.trenoescooter.com) on the Piazza del Cinquecento, which is in front of Termini station.

BIKING

Do not be surprised if you find a bike path that stops after a hundred yards: this is common and is an example of unsuccessful attempts to make the city more bike friendly. If you do rent a bike, be warned: traffic in the city is chaotic and can be difficult to navigate on two wheels.

Rome is built on several hills, so not every area is easily accessible on a bike. But many highlights in the historic center are on flat terrain, such as the neighborhoods around the Vatican, Piazza Navona, the Pantheon, Piazza del Popolo, Trevi Fountain, Campo de' Fiori, and the Ghetto.

There are relatively few bike lanes in Rome, especially in the city center. On www.piste-ciclabili.com you'll find an overview of all the paths (green lines). Want to enjoy a nice bike ride in the heart of the city without having to navigate heavy traffic? Go down to the riverside and ride the Lungotevere—a long path running along the riverbank. In the rest of the city, you have to be vigilant. The average Roman driver is not very attentive to cyclists. And in case your bell doesn't work, shout "Attenzione!" (watch out)! There are basically two rules to follow: wear a helmet and don't be in a hurry.

For bike rentals and tours, try Topbike Rental & Tours (Via Labicana 49, www.topbikerental.com, 06-4882893). The enthusiastic English-speaking staff here will gladly take you on a tour to introduce you to Rome and its rich history. You'll find many alternatives online such as Bici & Baci (www.bicibaci.com) and Bikeology (aroundrome.eu).

TOP 10 FILM & TV LOCATIONS

1 **Cinecittà** is an important film set > Via Tuscolana 1055

2 Anita Ekberg bathed in **Trevi Fountain** in *La Dolce Vita* > p. 106

3 **La Bocca della Verità** was featured in *Roman Holiday* > p. 67

4 Tom Cruise drove down the **Spanish Steps** in *Mission Impossible 7* > p. 106

5 Tom Hanks looked for *Angels & Demons* at **Piazza del Popolo** > p. 106

6 *The Young Pope* and *The New Pope* show the **Vatican** > p. 78

7 The *Suburra* neighborhood is now called **Monti** > p. 38

8 **Piazza Navona** appears in *Eat, Pray, Love* > p. 24

9 Some of *To Rome With Love* is in **Trastevere** > p. 119

10 *All the Money in the World* features **Mercati di Traiano** > p. 48

9

7

2

6

3

TOP 10 RESTAURANTS

1 **Armando al Pantheon** is almost as old as the temple itself > p. 70

2 **Come il Latte** serves the creamiest gelato > p. 109

3 Choices, choices at **Roscioli** > p. 25

4 Emperors would have eaten at **La Taverna dei Fori Imperiali** > p. 53

5 Enjoy a glass of natural wine at **Circoletto** > p. 71

6 Have an aperitivo among locals at **La Zanzara** > p. 88

7 The most delicious pizza is at **Salvatore** > p. 90

8 A great evening is guaranteed at **Osteria delle Coppelle** > p. 30

9 For kosher food go to **Su'Ghetto** > p. 70

10 **Siciliainbocca al Flaminio** has the best fish > p. 140

TOP 10 NIGHTLIFE

1. Have a late dinner at **Santo** in Trastevere > p. 130
2. Sip cocktails on the terrace of **Campo de' Fiori** > p. 36
3. Dance at **Emerald's Independent Bar**'s unplugged sessions > p. 89
4. Drinks start at 7pm at **Piazza della Madonna dei Monti** > p. 57
5. See a show in the old slaughterhouse **Mattatoio di Roma** > p. 124
6. You have many choices at **Ponte Milvio** > Roma Nord
7. Have an Aperol spritz at **Camillo dal 1890** > p. 30
8. Enjoy cocktails at **Blackmarket Hall** > p. 50
9. Visit the **Musei Vaticani** on Friday night > p. 82
10. Listen to live music on the square at **Bar San Calisto** > p. 130

TOP 10 SUNDAYS

1 After Sunday Mass, the Pope gives a blessing at **Piazza San Pietro** > p. 85

2 **Palatino** and **Foro Romano** are the heart of ancient Rome > p. 45

3 Antiquities come to life in **Ostia Antica** > Via dei Romagnoli 717

4 View the impressive Etruscan collection at **Villa Giulia** > Piazzale di Villa Giulia 9

5 Brunch is served at the **Chiostro del Bramante** > p. 22

6 Swim in **Lago di Bracciano** > p. 143

7 See the beach in **Fregene** > p. 142

8 Find vintage clothing at **Borghetto Flaminio** > Piazza della Marina

9 Museums such as **Castel Sant'Angelo** are free the first Sunday of each month > p. 86

10 Explore the fabulous **Quartiere Coppedè** > p. 141

WALK 1

VIA GIULIA, CAMPO DE' FIORI & PIAZZA NAVONA

ABOUT THE WALK

If you've never been to Rome before, this walk is a must. It will take you down the most beautiful streets, across the most attractive squares and bridges, past the most impressive churches and the nicest stores, and to the finest terraces and tastiest restaurants. Feel free to take a small detour or walk an extra lap if a view strikes your fancy—you can't go wrong in these neighborhoods.

THE NEIGHBORHOODS

This walk unfolds along the grand Renaissance street **Via Giulia** (named after Pope Julius II) on the east side of the Tiber River. At its southern end, you'll exit under a Michelangelo-designed arch, cross to the west side of the Tiber, and tour a small section of the Trastevere neighborhood. Then you'll cross the river again toward **Campo de' Fiori** and Piazza Navona in the Centro Storico (old center)—a dense maze of cobblestoned roads, charming shops, and eateries. During the Roman Republic this area was the heart of commerce, religion, and culture, and it has always stayed that way. It was the only part of Rome that remained inhabited after the collapse of the Roman Empire. Here you can just walk into a church (there are many along Via Giulia) and see frescoes by Raphael and paintings by Caravaggio, then you can relax and enjoy a plate of pasta outside with an Aperol spritz in hand.

One of the most beautiful and oldest streets on this walk is **Via dei Coronari,** named after the rosary merchants in the area, who sold their wares to the thousands of pilgrims who passed by every day on their way to the Vatican. Although the street dates to ancient Rome, it has a real Renaissance character, thanks to Pope Sixtus who gave the Coronari a major overhaul in the 15th century. This authentically Roman street has shops and plenty of cozy coffee bars and restaurants.

WALK 1 DESCRIPTION (approx. 4 mi/6 km)

Start beneath the stars at Arco dei Banchi 1. Walk down the street, turn left, cross Corso Vittoria Emanuele II, and turn right onto Via Acciaiolo for a vegan snack 2. Walk back a bit and turn right onto Piazza dell'Oro for Via Giulia 3. Turn right on Vicolo della Scimia and walk left up Via Bravaria to cross the river. Take a left down the stairs to Via della Lungara. To the right on Via Corsini is an oasis of tranquility 4. Continue along Via della Lungara, under Porto Settimania, and walk left on Via di Santa Dorotea. Continue straight to Via Benedetta and turn left onto Piazza Trilussa. Walk over the Ponte Sisto 5 and go straight on Via dei Pettinari for a little store 6 and gallery 7. Continue to Via dei Giubbonari, and turn right here for clothes 8 and for some goodies 9. Turn around, enter Largo dei Librari for mini-pizzas 10, or walk to Campo de' Fiori 11 12. Take Via del Baullari to a restaurant 13 and Palazzo Farnese 14. To the right of the palazzo take Via di Monserrato, turn right again on Via di Montoro, then turn left on Via del Pellegrino 15 16. Walk to Via dei Bancchi Vecchi for street food 17 and a glass of wine 18. Turn right on Via Sforza Cesarini, cross Corso Vittorio Emanuele, and continue straight. Cross Piazza dell'Orologio to Via degli Orsini and take a left on Via di Panico. At Piazza dei Coronari, turn right on Via dei Coronari for special stores and gelato 19 20 21 22 23. Walk straight for a long time and turn right on Via Arco delle Pace 24 for a lunch place 25. Continue until you reach the charming Via del Governo Vecchio and have a gelato 26. Turn around and continue on Via del Governo Vecchio 27. Walk past the "talking" statue to Piazza Navona 28. Take it all in 29 30 before you settle down among the Romans 31. Turn right down the square in front of a magic toy store 32 and walk right around the bend to turn left onto Via di Santa Giovanna d'Arco. At the Largo Giuseppe Toniolo square, turn left on Via della Scrofa for jewelry 33. Turn right on Via della Stelletta for a souvenir 34. There are two options for a delicious meal: left on Via Metastasio 35 or follow the street to the right for Via delle Coppelle 36. Turn right to Via della Maddalena. Cross the little square, take a right, and walk straight, crossing Piazza Rondanini. You are back at Largo Giuseppe Toniolo, but this time turn left to visit a church 37. Cross Piazza di Sant'Eustachio and turn right on Via dei Sediari. On the corner is the perfect bar to finish your walk 38.

SIGHTS & ATTRACTIONS

1 The **Arco dei Banchi** is more of a passageway than an actual arch and connects Via del Banco di Santo Spirito with Via Paola. The Italian banker and Renaissance patron Agostino Chigi lived in the palazzo next door, and this is where he built a wall to protect his private property. It has since been painted inside with a blue sky filled with stars. The oil painting of the Madonna dates to the 19th century, and the line across the stone at the entrance recalls the high-water mark of the 1277 Tiber flood.
Via dell'Arco dei Banchi, Bus to Acciaioli

5 The **Ponte Sisto** bridge was built by Pope Sixtus IV in the late 15th century. The previous bridge was the site of a disaster in 1450, which was a Holy Year. Foot traffic heading to Castel Sant'Angelo was so high that pilgrims crowded each other, and some fell into the Tiber and drowned. The new bridge was completed in time for the Holy Year 1475, and thus for the new influx of pilgrims.
Ponte Sisto, Bus to Lgt Farnesina/Trilussa

14 The construction of the French **Palazzo Farnese** was commissioned in 1514 but had to pause when Holy Roman Emperor Charles V invaded Rome. A succession of architects worked on it, including Michelangelo, and today the building is considered the most important example of a high Renaissance palazzo in Rome.
Piazza Farnese, visite-palazzofarnese.it, open tours Mon & Wed 2:30, 3:30, 4:30pm, Fri 3:30, 4:30pm, Sat 4:30pm (make reservations in advance), tour €12, Bus to Corso Vittorio Emanuele/Navona

24 Named after its architect, Donanto Bramante, **Chiostro del Bramante** is characterized by the harmony, elegance, and proportions typical of Renaissance architecture. In the courtyard, check out the pilasters at the corners and the way they have disappeared into the wall. On the first floor, a colorful bistro makes for a unique spot for coffee or brunch. From the room next to the bar, you can see into Santa Maria della Pace and a fresco featuring sibyls painted by Raphael.
Arco della Pace 5, chiostrodelbramante.it, bistro open Mon-Fri 10am-8pm, Sat-Sun 10am-9pm, Bus to Senato

30

28 **Piazza Navona** was built on top the remains of Emperor Domitian's athletic stadium. North of the square and inside the crypt of the Sant'Agnese church in Agone, you can still see some remains of the stadium. Houses were built after the stadium was no longer in use, and in the 17th century, Pope Innocent X gave the square a facelift, which resulted in the construction of Borromini's Sant'Agnese church and Bernini's Fontana dei Quattro Fiumi.

Piazza Navona, Bus to Corso Vittorio Emanuele/Navona

29 According to legend, Saint Agnes was a Christian girl at a time when Christians in Rome were persecuted. Agnes was sentenced to death and burned at the stake for her beliefs at the spot where the church dedicated to her, **Sant'Agnese in Agone,** was built. With its undulating façade, the church is a beautiful example of the baroque architecture of Borromini. The dome features a depiction of Agnes being taken to heaven.

Piazza Navona/Via S. Maria dell'Anima 30A, santagneseinagone.org, open Tue-Fri 9am-1pm & 3-7pm Sat-Sun 9am-1pm & 3-8pm, free, Bus to Rinascimento

30 The **Fontana dei Quattro Fiumi,** in the middle of Piazza Navona, was designed by Bernini, a small miracle given the rivalry between the Bernini family and the family of Pope Innocent X who commissioned the renovation of the plaza. The fountain is a symbol for the four most important rivers in the 17th century: the Nile (the figure with the cloth over his head), the Ganges (the figure with the oar), the Danube (the figure with his hand on the coat of arms), and the Rio Plata (the figure with a stack of coins).

Piazza Navona, Bus to Corso Vittorio Emanuele/Navona

37 **San Luigi dei Francesi** conceals an interior of Baroque excess. Don't miss the three paintings by Caravaggio in the back chapel on the left. Subdued and dark, yet intense and theatrical, they depict the life of Matthew.

Piazza San Luigi dei Francesi 5, saintlouis-rome.net, open Mon-Fri 9:30am-12:45pm & 2:30-6:30pm, Sat 9:30am-12:15pm & 2:30-6:30pm, Sun 11:30am-12:45pm & 2:30-6:30pm, free, Bus to Senato

FOOD & DRINK

2 You can drink coffee—caffé—in Rome endlessly, standing at the counter in an authentic little bar, and you must do it at least once. And if you need a cappuccino with homemade almond milk in a pleasant environment, **Écru** is the place to go. It's also a great spot for lunch or dinner. Everything is vegetarian!

Via Acciaioli 13, tel. 06-68804282, ecrurawfood.it, open Mon-Thu 10am-10pm, Fri 10am-11pm, cappuccino €3.50, Bus to Via Paola

9 For three generations Roscioli on Via dei Chiavari has provided Romans with the best pizza bianca and other breads. Now nearby **Roscioli Salumeria con Cucino,** just around the corner, is proving to be an even bigger hit. The shop sells fantastic cheeses, hams, and wines, and the restaurant offers various cheese and charcuterie platters, which are a lot of fun. Reservations are a must, especially for dinner.

Via dei Giubbonari 21, tel. 06-6875287, salumeriaroscioli.com, shop open daily 9am-9pm, restaurant open daily 12:30-3:30pm & 7-11pm, pasta €19, Tram 8 Arenula/Cairoli

⑩ You can find round pizzas or pizza al taglio (rectangular) everywhere, but **Amerina la Pizzetta** serves mini pan pizzas. Amerina is the name of the owners' grandmother who is from Abruzzo, where mini pizzas are a traditional regional dish. They span 7 inches (18 cm)—still big enough to try a few with different toppings.

Largo dei Librari 82, tel. 06-45495604, amerinalapizzetta.it, open Tue-Thu 6pm-midnight, Sat noon-1am, Sun 11am-1am, pizza €4.50, Tram 8 Arenula/Cairoli

⑫ If you don't feel like sitting down for an elaborate dinner, try pizza al taglio or pizza bianca at **Forno Campo de' Fiori.** Everything is made fresh daily. This bakery has been a phenomenon in Rome for thirty years, so it's no wonder there's always a line out the door. Are you visiting around Christmastime? Try a panettone.

Piazza Campo de' Fiori 22, tel. 06-68806662, fornocampodefiori.com, open daily 7:30am-2:30pm & 4:45-8pm, panino €4, Bus to Corse Vittorio Emanuele/Navona

⑬ Vino meets boutique is the concept at **VyNIQUE Farnese.** The interior combines a traditional Italian bar with an eclectic twist. If you'd like a bit more for breakfast than cappuccino and a cornetto, they serve brunch until late in the evening, but you can also opt for pasta.

Via dei Baullari 106, tel. 331-336-6185, vynique.it, open Mon-Thu 7:30am-11pm, Fri-Sun 7:30am-midnight, €13, Bus to Corso Vittorio Manuele/Navona

⑯ **Barnum** is one of those places that's constantly buzzing. Locals come in for a quick coffee, and some people sit and work on the bench across from the bar or at the large table in the back—at least until lunch when the place gets packed. Try the avocado toast or eggs Benedict. And if you're lucky, you'll get a table outside.

Via del Pellegrino 87, tel. 06-64760483, open daily 8am-3:30pm, €12, Bus to Corse Vittorio Emanuele/Navona

17
SUPPLIZIO
CIBO DI STRADA

21
ELATERIA DEL TEATR
STICCERIA CIOCCOLAT

9

17

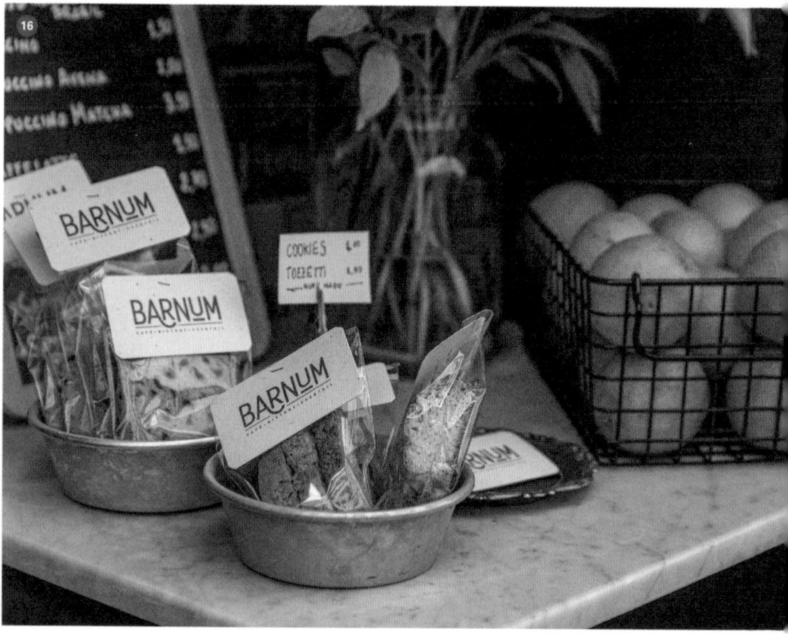

16

21

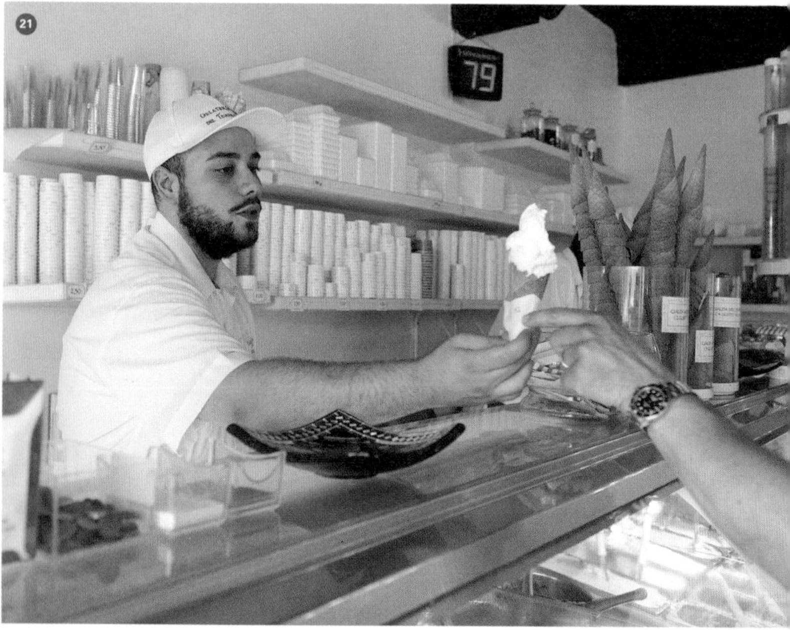

17 You cannot leave Rome without having tasted supplì. At **Supplizio,** these classic risotto balls are filled with ragù and buffalo mozzarella and are made according to their own recipe.

Via dei Banchi Vecchi 143, tel. 06-89871920, supplizioroma.it, open Mon-Sat noon-3:30pm & 5-9:30pm, supplì €3, Bus to Chiesa Nuova

18 **Il Goccetto** ("the sip") has the warm and comfy atmosphere of a cozy café. The walls are covered with rows of wine bottles. Their wine list is extensive, and if you can't decide, choose something from the featured items on the chalkboard. You can't have a full meal here, but some snacks are on offer.

Via dei Banchi Vecchi 14, tel. 06-99448583, open Mon 5pm-midnight, Tue-Sat noon-midnight, glass wine €7, Bus to Chiesa Nuova

21 **Gelateria del Teatro** features flavors based on the season. All ingredients are organic and artisanal: lemons from Amalfi, pistachio from Sicily, blackberries from Tolva, chocolate from Peru. Strawberry is the only flavor that's available year-round, to the delight of the local elementary school kids.

Via dei Coronari 65/66, tel. 06-45474880, gelateriadelteatro.it, open daily noon-9pm, gelato €3.50, Bus to Lgt Tor di Nona/Rondinella

25 The menu at **Ruma Bottega & Cucina** is full of seasonal dishes prepared with produce from the family farm in the Maremma region. Brother Guido and sister Matidia call this place a farm-to-table bistro for a reason. Think cheeses made with Maremma buffalo milk, meat from the local pasture, and vegetables from their own garden.

Via di Parione 13, tel. 06-89471435, rumabottegaecucina.com, open Tue-Sun 11am-11pm, €10, Bus to Corso Vittorio Emanuele/Navona

30 An Italian gelato covered in melted white or pure chocolate—that's what you get at creamery **Frigidarium.** Besides the standard flavors, there are the shop's specialties. Try the Mozart—a combination of almond, pistachio, and chocolate gelato. They also have gluten-free cones.

Via del Governo Vecchio 112, tel. 06-31052934, frigidariumgelateria.com, open daily 10:30-1am, 2 scoops €2.50, Bus to Corso Vittorio Emanuele/Navona

31 When Romans go to Piazza Navona, they stop at **Camillo dal 1890** for a drink. The bar was opened by the last generation's great-grandfather, but recently the menu was given a contemporary twist, and the interior was updated to its current pink splendor. You won't find any waiters standing outside to lure you in; just get a drink at the bar and enjoy.

Piazza Navona 79-81, tel. 06-56558161, camillopiazzanavona.it, open Mon-Thu 10-1am, Fri-Sat 9-3am, Sun 9-1:30am, spritz €9, pasta €15, Bus to Senato

35 In a historic building from the 1930s, you will find what appears to be a typical Roman restaurant. **CiPASSO Bistrot** proves that tradition and contemporary creativity go well together. Their dishes are traditional Italian with a modern twist, such as cacio e pepe paired with walnuts and pear. The walls are filled with countless bottles of wine—they have as many as 150 labels—and antique signs.

Via Metastasio 21, tel. 06-68892620, cipassoitalia.it, open Mon-Thu 6-11pm, Fri-Sun noon-3:30pm & 6-11pm, €22, Metro to Spagna

36 When the market vendors leave, the terrace at **Osteria delle Coppelle** opens and fills up almost immediately. Start with panzerotti, formaggi, and salumi, and take your time picking your main course. A favorite is tagliolini al tartufo (pasta with black truffles). Inside it feels like an Italian living room.

Piazza delle Coppelle 54, tel. 06-45502826, osteriadellecoppelle.com, open daily 12:30pm-2am, €18, Bus to Prefetti

38 To end this walk with a bang, stop at the trendy cocktail bar **LIÒN.** You can come here throughout the day, but it really comes to life in the evening. Order a cocktail and keep an eye on social media for any weekend events.

Largo della Sapienza 1, tel. 06-81157070, open Mon-Thu & Sun 10-1am, Fri-Sat 10-2am, cocktail €13, Bus to Corse Vittorio Emanuele/Navona

SHOPPING

6 **Lela** is a cute shop with a Scandinavian vibe and tons of little knickknacks—pressed flowers, kitchen linen, ceramic plates and cups, and all kinds of kitchen utensils.

Via dei Pettinari 37, open daily 11am-7pm, Bus to Lgt Vallati/Pettinari

8 **104 Pandemonium** has two floors of beautiful clothing from Italian and international brands for both men and women. The styles vary from casual daywear to fancy long-Roman-nights-out wear.

Via dei Giubbonari 104, 104pandemonium.it, open daily 10am-8pm, Tram 8 Arenula/Cairoli

15 At **Officine ReD** you won't be shopping for fast fashion flimsy stuff. Here, they sell high-quality, beautiful, and simple yet unique clothing, shoes, and accessories. Men and women can shop here for stunning Italian brands, such as Aspesi, Palto, and OA non fashion.

Via del Pellegrino 79, open Mon-Sat 10:30am-8pm, Sun 11am-8pm, Bus to Corso Vittorio Emanuele/Navona

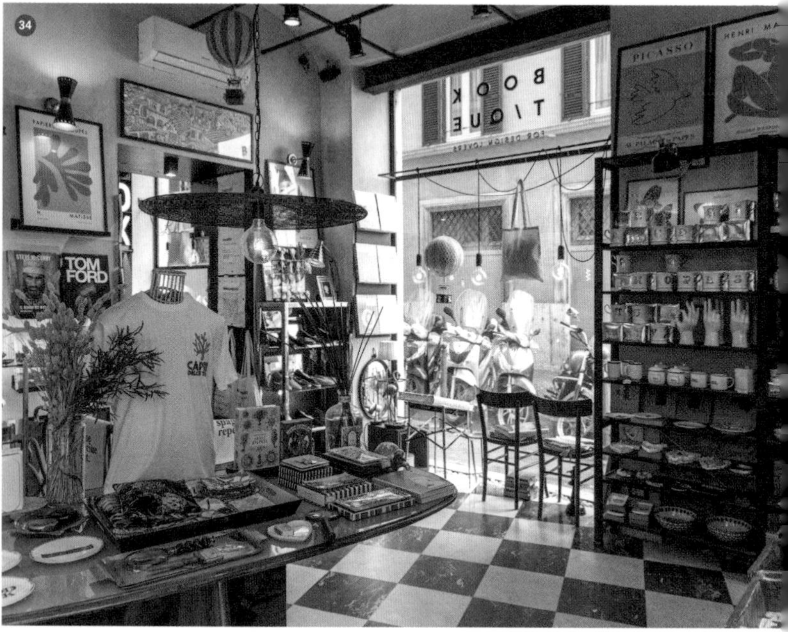

34

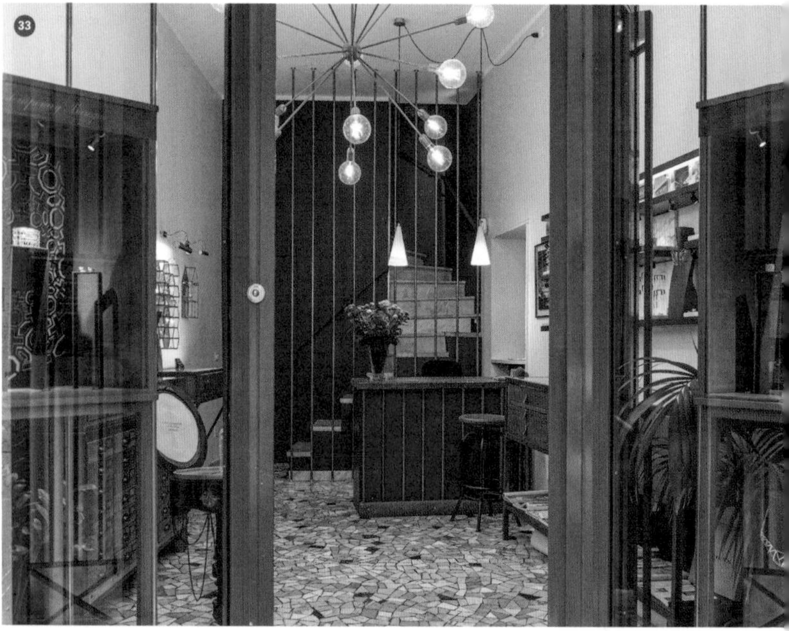

33

19 Romans like to look their best, which means you might sometimes feel somewhat underdressed with your sneakers and backpack. Go to **Marta Ray** and your problem is fixed in no time at all. They sell elegant flats, beautiful sandals, and great bags in many colors.

Via dei Coronari 150, martaray.it, open daily 10:30am-7:30pm, Bus to Lgt Tor di Nona/ Rondinella

20 This shop undoubtedly comes as a surprise, but we want to share it with you, nonetheless. The **Rome Duck Store** sells rubber ducks in all shapes, sizes, and colors—superhero ducks, celebrity ducks, even a Colosseum duck. The playful shop forms a stark contrast with the historical street where it is located.

Via dei Coronari 108, romeduckstore.it, open daily 10:30am-7:30pm, Bus to Lgt Tor di Nona/Rondinella

22 Gallery **Gioielli a Roma** located on Via dei Coronari is currently run by a third generation of the Borrazzi family. Their signet rings refer to Italy's cultural and historical heritage. They also sell bracelets, necklaces, and cufflinks.

Via dei Coronari 32, grandtourcollection.com, open Mon-Sat 9:30am-8pm, Bus to Senato

23 The white walls of **Essenzialmente di Laura** are lined with antique, dark wood cabinets full of fragrances. All the scents are displayed in special tubes, giving it a bit of a laboratory vibe. The owner, Laura Bosetti Tonatto, is well known in the perfume industry, having created collections for Queen Elizabeth II and the famous brand La Bottega. More importantly, all the scents smell amazing.

Via dei Coronari 57, essenzialmentelaura.it, open daily 11am-7pm, Bus to Senato

32 **Al Sogno,** or "the dream," is a toyshop for young and old. The name of the shop is chosen perfectly because it is a dream of a shop. Step into the magical world of countless stuffed animals, old-fashioned toys, dolls, music boxes, and elves, or go in search of Pinocchio.

Piazza Navona 53, alsogno.com, open daily 10am-8pm, Bus to Corso Vittorio Emanuele/Navona

33 Jewelry based on Roman landmarks—sounds like something that could go incredibly wrong. Yet here it has succeeded. The silversmiths at **Co.Ro.** create jewelry that is special and striking yet has something subtle about it. Any references to the Colosseum, for example, are never too literal: you see it only if you know it.

Via della Scrofa 52, corojewels.com, open Mon-Sat 10:30am-7:30pm, Sun 2:30-7:30pm, Bus to Senato

34 In addition to unusual books at **Booktique,** you'll also find fun notebooks, canvas bags, pens, water bottles, tasteful accessories, and delightful, geeky knickknacks. What you go in for are the souvenirs in the form of magnets, mugs, canvas bags with Roman sayings like "Ahó, Eccallà" or "Se lallero." The translation is added, too.

Via della Stelletta 17, booktique.info, open daily 11am-7pm, Bus to Senato

MORE TO EXPLORE

3 When Pope Julius II wasn't busy having Michelangelo paint the Sistine Chapel and refurbishing St. Peter's Basilica, he worked on easing the ever-growing flow of pilgrims to the Vatican. The result was **Via Giulia.** Designed by Bramante, this is Rome's loveliest Renaissance street.

Via Giulia, Bus to Corso Vittorio Emanuele/Tassoni

4 With a 12-acre park and about 20,000 square feet (2,000 sq m) of greenhouses, **Orto Botanico** is one of the largest gardens in Italy. Currently it holds more than three thousand species of plants. You will find a bamboo forest, a rose garden, several palm trees, a Japanese garden, monumental trees, and a butterfly house.

Largo Cristina di Svezia 23A-24, web.uniroma1.it/ortobotanico/en, open daily 9am-6:30pm (last entry 5:30pm), €5, Bus to Piazza della Rovere

33

34
TOM FORD
CAPRI

15

15

15
79
OfficineReD
OfficineReD

8

7 The **Dorothy Circus Gallery** contrasts somewhat with traditional Roman museums, but it is a hysterically fun place. Stroll through the dark red corridors, and a world of pop iconography, surrealism, and magical realism will open before you. The exhibitions of international established and emerging artists are refreshing. To visit the gallery you must have a reservation.

Via dei Pettinari 76, dorothycircusgallery.com, open Sat noon-7pm, free, Bus to Lgt Vallati/Pettinari

11 **Campo de' Fiori** is one of the most vibrant squares in Rome. Stroll through the market during the day or come for aperitivo at one of the eateries with tables on the plaza. Overlooking the square is an imposing statue of Giordano Bruno, the philosopher and cosmologist who was sentenced to death for heresy here in 1600.

Piazza Campo de' Fiori, Bus to Corso Vittorio Emanuele/Navona

27 **Via del Governo Vecchio** connects Piazza dell'Orologio with Piazza di Pasquino. The street is named after Governo Vecchio ("old government") because until 1755 the papal government was located in a palazzo on the street; at number 39 to be exact. At number 66, you will find probably the smallest house in Rome. Check out Ciao Vintage on number 71, one of the better vintage shops. At number 104 is a beautiful lawyer's palace where the façade is decorated with statues of famous lawyers.

Via del Governo Vecchio, Bus to Corso Vittorio Emanuele/Navona

WALK 2

COLOSSEUM & MONTI

ABOUT THE WALK

This walk passes by two papal basilicas, through the spiritual and official center of Roman antiquity, and then over the Capitoline—one of Rome's seven hills that was the center of power during the Renaissance. Then you'll visit the charming neighborhood of Monti, which is now one of the most popular areas where Romans come to shop and drink.

THE NEIGHBORHOODS

Here you will find the San Giovanni in Laterano—Rome's cathedral that, unlike St. Peter's, you can often enter without standing in line. The **Colosseum** is probably on your to-do list, so take in the view of it from **Parco del Colle Oppio** before descending the hill and getting a closer look at the colossal amphitheater.

The **Foro Romano** was the political, commercial, and religious heart of the Roman Empire. This is where the senate would meet and politicians would deliver their speeches. Merchants came here to do business, priests made offerings, and people shopped for goods and talked about the latest news. Julius Caesar, Augustus, Vespasian, Nerva, and Trajan each had their own forum built, complete with temples: the **Fori Imperiali.**

Piazza del Campidoglio was designed by Michelangelo, and to impress Emperor Charles V, who had so brutally invaded Rome a few years earlier, this square had to be as magnificent as possible. The emperor even had to be able to climb the stairs on horseback. In the center is a replica of the equestrian statue of Marcus Aurelius. The original is on display in the **Musei Capitolini** adjacent to the square, and so is the iconic Lupa with Romulus and Remus.

In ancient Rome, the place where you would have found the Suburra (suburb) is now the **Monti** (mountains) district. It was separated from the Fori by a thick, fireproof wall. Monti is now a beautiful area and full of character. There are small streets with shiny sampietrini (the sidewalk tiles), lush ivy, and flowering plants over the façades of the many bars. This centrally located neighborhood is home to fantastic antique stores and fine boutiques that you'll love. When you've spent a few hours in the afternoon at the Foro Romano, Palatino, and the Colosseum, your aperitivo awaits just around the corner in Piazza della Madonna dei Monti.

SHORT ON TIME? HERE ARE THE HIGHLIGHTS:

6 SAN PIETRO IN VINCOLI + 7 COLOSSEUM + 10 PALATINO/MUSEO PALATINO + 12 FORI IMPERIALI + 21 PIAZZA DELLA MADONNA DEI MONTI

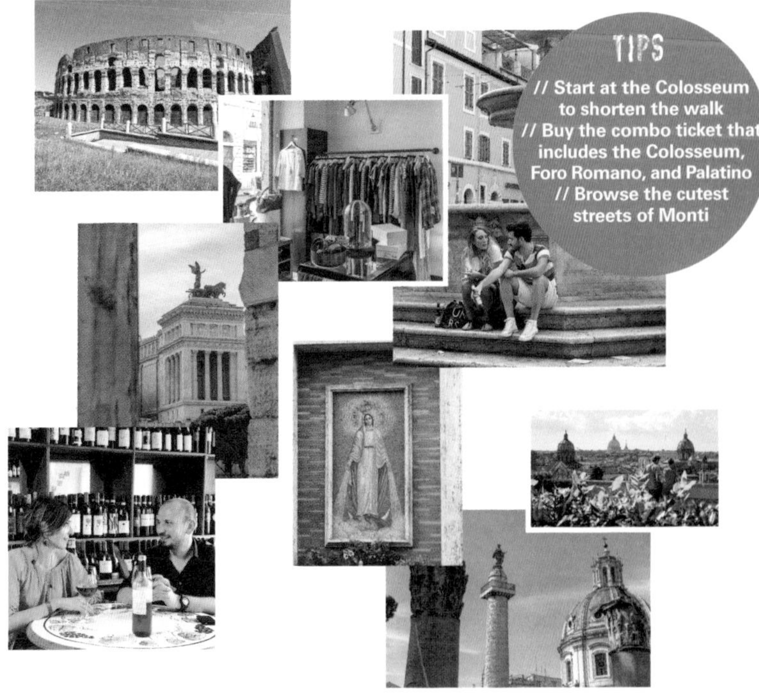

COLOSSEUM & MONTI

1. Materia
2. San Giovanni in Laterano/ Scala Santa
3. 081 Café
4. Pasticceria Cipriani
5. Parco del Colle Oppio
6. **San Pietro in Vincoli**
7. **Colosseum**
8. Via Sacra
9. Arco di Constantino
10. **Palatino/Museo Palatino**
11. Foro Romano
12. **Fori Imperiali**
13. Arco di Settimio Severo
14. Piazza del Campidoglio/ Musei Capitolini
15. Terrazza Caffarelli
16. Vittoriano/Museo del Risorgimento
17. Colonna di Traiano
18. Mercati di Traiano
19. Arco dei Pantani
20. Al42
21. **Piazza della Madonna dei Monti**
22. Ce Stamo a Pensà
23. Hang Roma
24. Antigallery
25. LOL
26. Elena Kihlman Design
27. Gelateria S.M.Maggiore
28. Santa Maria Maggiore
29. Blackmarket Hall
30. Kokoro
31. Ai Tre Scalini
32. Candle Store
33. Pifebo Vintage Shop
34. Al Vino Al Vino
35. La Casetta a Monti
36. Pizzeria alle Carrette
37. La Taverna dei Fori Imperiali

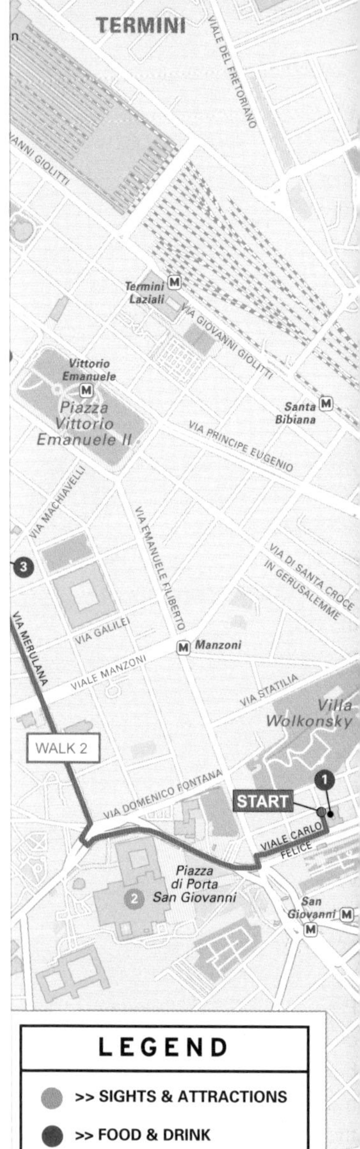

WALK 2 DESCRIPTION (approx. 6 mi/9 km)

Start with breakfast or lunch on Via Andrea Provana 1. Walk to Viale Carlo Felice, turn right, and walk toward the end of the street to visit the basilica 2. Walk to the right of the basilica, pass the obelisk, and turn right onto Via Merulana for coffee 3. Walk back a bit to turn right on Via Guicciardarini and take the first right on Via Carlo Botta for cookies 4. Walk straight ahead and meander through the Parco del Colle Oppio 5. Exit the park on Via delle Sette Sale and see Michelangelo's Moses 6. Turn left on Via degli Annibaldi and walk toward the Colosseum 7. Walk right along there for the most important street from ancient Rome 8 and the Arco di Constantino 9. Walk farther up the hill, where the imperial palace once stood 10. Go back down past the Colosseum and turn left on Via dei Fori Imperiali. On the left you can see the Foro Romano, once the center of the city 11. Several emperors added their Fori Imperiali on the right 12. Turn left up Via di San Pietro in Carcere. From behind the Arco di Settimio Severo 13, there is a beautiful view. Walk to Piazza del Campidoglio and the Musei Capitolini 14. Enjoy a drink with a view in the museum café 15. Walk to the Monumento a Vittorio Emanuele II 16 on Piazza Venezia, which can be seen from the entire city. Cross over to Foro Traiano to find the Colonna di Traiano 17. Here you will find a complex of stores and market halls 18. Turn right on Via Magnanapoli, Via Quattro Novembre, Largo Magnanapoli, Salita del Grillo, and Via Tor de' Conti. Enjoy the view from Arco dei Pantani 19. Turn left on Via Baccina for the best pasta in Monti 20. Continue to the heart of Monti 21 22. Walk along Via degli Zingari for a leather bag 23 or an exhibition and a beer 24. Walk around the bend to Via Urbana for more stores 25 26. Turn right on Via delle Vasche and turn left on Via Cavour. Take a short break with gelato 27 and turn right at the piazza to visit the basilica 28. Walk around the basilica, turn left on Via di Santa Maria Maggiore, and walk back into Monti for a cocktail on Via Panisperna 29. On the second street on the right you will find the authentic Via del Boschetto where you can do some nice shopping 30. Walk back slightly and have a glass of wine a little farther on 31. Turn left on Via dei Serpenti for even more stores and wine 32 33 34. Turn right on Via della Madonna dei Monti to end the day 35 36 37.

SIGHTS & ATTRACTIONS

2 **San Giovanni in Laterano** is the oldest church in the city. The church was founded in the 4th century by Emperor Constantine, and in the mid-17th century, Baroque architect Francesco Borromini designed the basilica you see today, preserving older elements whenever possible and incorporating them into the newer Baroque structure. Next to the cathedral, opposite the square with the Egyptian obelisk, are the Holy Steps or the **Scala Santa.** According to legend, Christ walked on these before his crucifixion. Pilgrims ascend the stairs on their knees, hoping for mercy.

Piazza di San Giovanni in Laterano, turismoroma.it/it/luoghi/basilica-di-san-giovanni-laterano, cathedral open daily 7am-6:30pm, Scala Santa Mon-Sat 6am-2pm & 3-6:30pm, Sun 7am-2pm & 3-6:30pm, cathedral free, Scala Santa €6, Metro A, C San Giovanni, Tram 3, 8 Porta S. Giovanni/Carlo Felice

6 The church **San Pietro in Vincoli** is where the chains (Latin: *vincola*) that were used to restrain Saint Peter during his imprisonment in the Mamertine Prison in Rome were kept, making it a destination for pilgrims. The columns in the church are antique—that is, reused from other structures. The tomb of Pope Julius II, located on the right at the back of the church, is the highlight of the basilica and features Michelangelo's statue of Moses, which, due to a mistranslation in the Bible, has horns instead of radiant skin.

Piazza San Pietro in Vincoli 4a, lateranensi.org/sanpietroinvincoli, open daily 8am-12:30pm & 3-6pm, free, Metro B, B1 Colosseo, Tram 3, 8 Piazza del Colosseo

7 The opening of the **Colosseum** in 80 CE was celebrated with games that lasted one hundred days and one hundred nights. There were all different kinds of tournaments, from gladiator fights to hunting parties and probably even sea battles. Underneath the arena was an intricate system of chambers, corridors, and elevators that allowed a wild animal to suddenly appear in the arena. The sheer scale of the Colosseum and the pace at which it was built set it apart from similar structures of its time.

Piazza del Colosseo 1, colosseo.it, open daily 8:30am to sunset, entrance Combi ticket with Palatino & Forum Romanum €16, Metro B, B1 Colosseo, Tram 3, 8 Piazza del Colosseo

17

2

14

8 **Via Sacra** was the most important street in the city center of ancient Rome. Generals who had won a war could make a request to the Roman Senate for a victory parade here. However, there were a few requirements: they needed to have conquered a significant amount of new territory and killed at least five thousand enemy soldiers. During the parade, prisoners of war marched through the street, and spoils of war were put on display. Finally, the enemy leader was executed in public.

Part of Foro Romano, Metro B, B1 Colosseo, Tram 3, 8 Piazza del Colosseo

9 The **Arco di Costantino** was built in 315 CE in honor of Emperor Constantine, who liberated Rome from the tyrant Maxentius. The triumphal arch is ornately decorated, but only the smallest reliefs alongside the edges refer to Emperor Constantine. The rest relates to the reigns of other leaders, such as Trajan, Hadrian, and Marcus Aurelius.

Between Via di San Gregorio & Piazza del Colosseo, Metro B, B1 Colosseo, Tram 3, 8 Piazza del Colosseo

10 Archaeological excavations on **Palatino** (Palatine Hill) revealed settlements that have been here since the beginning of the Iron Age. During the time of the Roman Republic, the elite lived on this hill, and during the Roman Empire gigantic palaces were built here. In the **Museo Palatino** you can view remnants of frescos, statues, bas-reliefs, and other objects found on the hill. And after many restorations the house of Augustus, Casa di Augusto, is now also open to the public.

Parco Archeologico del Colosseo, colosseo.it/area/musei/museo-palatino, Palatino open daily 8:30am to sunset, entrance Combi ticket with Colosseum & Foro Romano €16, Metro B, B1 Colosseo, Tram 3, 8 Piazza del Colosseo

11 The **Foro Romano** (Roman Forum) was the most important center of the city. Little is left of most temples and buildings, but you get a good idea of the structure. Vesta, the virgin goddess of the hearth, was incredibly important in ancient Rome, and so was the small Tempio di Vesta; it was thought that Rome would perish if the sacred fire in the temple went out. The six Vestal Virgins who lived in the Casa delle Vestali were tasked with keeping the fire burning. Emperor Antoninus Pius had the Tempio di Antonino e Faustina built in honor of his late wife, Faustina. When he himself died, the temple was also dedicated to him. In the 8th century, the Romans rebuilt the temple into a church, using the ancient columns as an entrance.

Via Della Salara Vecchia 5/6, colosseo.it/en/area/the-roman-forum, open daily 9am-7pm, entrance Combi ticket with Colosseum & Palatino €16, Metro B, B1 Colosseo, Tram 3, 8 Piazza del Colosseo

12 When Rome became an empire and the city rapidly expanded, it didn't take long for the central square Foro Romano to become too small. Hence the **Fori Imperiali** (Imperial Forums) were built. In 54 BCE, Julius Caesar founded the first forum, and his adopted son followed fifty years later with the Forum of Augustus. Emperor Trajan built the biggest imperial forum of all: it borders the market that he also commissioned.

Via dei Fori Imperiali, colosseo.it/en/tickets/forum-pass-super-ticket, open daily 9am-4:30pm, entrance at Foro Romano, Fori Imperiali & Palatino €16, Metro B, B1 Colosseo, Tram 8 Venezia

13 As you wind your way up Via di San Pietro in Carcree to Piazza del Campidoglio, you will have the best view of the Foro Romano: you will feel so close to the **Arco di Settimio Severo**—triumphal arch of Septimius Severus—that you'll want to touch it. The arch was built in 203 CE to commemorate the tenth anniversary of Emperor Severus's victory over the Parthians (an Indo-Iranian people), which isn't very old relative to the nearby temples that date to the 5th century BCE.
Part of Foro Romano

14 The Capitolini is the smallest of the seven hills. In designing **Piazza del Campidoglio,** Michelangelo had to pull out all the stops to make it look as big as possible. Just look at how small the statues on the eaves are. The equestrian statue in the center is an exact copy of a 2nd century statue of Marcus Aurelius. The original can be found in the **Musei Capitolini,** located in the two palaces on the left and right of the square. Other highlights not to be missed are the Lupa Capitolina, the remains of a colossal statue of Emperor Constantine, the Thorn Puller, Amor and Psyche, and the Dying Gaul.
Piazza del Campidoglio 1, museicapitolini.org, open daily 9:30am-7:30pm, entrance €17, Metro B, B1 Cavour, Tram 8 Venezia

15 The gigantic white patriotic monument commemorating the first king of Italy, Vittorio Emanuele II, **Vittoriano** on Piazza Venezia was built to celebrate the unification of Italy. Many Romans see it as an eyesore, and they mockingly call it "The Wedding Cake" or "The Typewriter." The building is impressive for its sheer size. The equestrian statue is so large that a dinner was held in the belly of the horse to celebrate its impending completion. The Vittoriano is home to the **Museo del Risorgimento,** which is dedicated to the century before the unification.
Piazza Venezia, vive.cultura.gov.it, open daily 9:30am-7pm, €16, Metro B, B1 Cavour, Tram 8 Venezia

13

⑰ Built in 113 CE, the **Colonna di Traiano** (Trajan's Column) is decorated with reliefs that tell of the battles Emperor Trajan waged in Dacia (currently Romania). With his spoils of war, Trajan was able to finance the construction of his forum. The column is as high as the hill that had to be excavated to build Trajan's Market.

Via dei Fori Imperiali, colosseo.it/area/colonna-traiana, Metro B, B1 Cavour, Tram 8 Venezia

⑱ During the reign of Emperor Trajan, at the start of the 2nd century CE, Rome underwent a period of growth and prosperity. The **Mercati di Traiano** (Trajan's Markets) gives us a glimpse of what daily life was like then. This enormous complex of 150 shops and offices is very well preserved—a testament to the work of architect Appollodoris of Damascus faced. The five floors of the market were made of brick-lined concrete to keep the steep hillside behind it—which had been excavated to build the fori—from collapsing.

Via Quattro Novembre 94, mercatiditraiano.it, open daily 9:30am-7:30m, €13, Metro B, B1 Cavour, Tram 8 Venezia

28 **Santa Maria Maggiore** is one of the four papal basilicas in Rome. The building is an embodiment of the city's long history: ancient Roman columns were part of the construction; the nave is from the original 5th century structure; the bell tower—which, at 245 feet (75 m) high, is the tallest in Rome—is from the 14th century; and there are chapels from the 16th and 17th centuries. The basilica is also called Our Lady of Snow. According to legend, Mary caused it to snow here in the middle of summer and later came to a pious couple as a vision telling them to build a church for her on this very spot. Bernini's grave is located behind the church.

Piazza di Santa Maria Maggiore, vatican.va, open daily 7am-6:45pm, free, Metro B, B1 Cavour, Tram 5, 14 Farini

FOOD & DRINK

1 Walk into **Materia** and you'll notice straight away that the Nordic trend has also hit Rome. Everything is light, clean, and responsibly sourced. It is a nice place to start your day with breakfast on the terrace, but you can also come here for lunch or appetizers. It's a small but varied menu.

Via Andrea Provana 7, tel. 06-56303156, materiacafe.com, open Mon 8am-4pm, Tue-Fri 8am-midnight, Sat-Sun 9am-midnight, coffee €1.10, lunch €13, Metro A, C San Giovanni, Tram 3, 8 Porta S. Giovanni/Carlo Felice

3 **081 Café** is the perfect stop for a traditional Italian breakfast: coffee and a cornetto con crema. A simple cup of Neapolitan coffee is also a favorite. The pastries are always fresh, and the staff is friendly and welcoming.

Via Merulana 83, tel. 340-339-7933, open Mon-Sat 8am-7pm, Sun 8:30am-1pm, coffee €1.50, Metro Vittorio Emanuele, Tram 5, 14 Vittorio Emanuele

15 **Terrazza Caffarelli** is housed inside the Musei Capitolini, although you can come here without visiting a museum. Having a cup of coffee on the more upscale terrace is well worth it; the panoramic view of Rome from here is spectacular.

Piazzale Caffarelli 4, tel. 06-69190564, terrazzacaffarelli.it, open daily 9:30am-7pm, coffee €3.50 sandwich €9.00, Metro B, B1 Cavour, Tram 8 Venezia

20 Pasta meets street food is the concept at **Al42.** Don't expect table linens or a three-course meal but do expect some of the best pasta in Monti. They don't take reservations and seating inside is limited, but you usually don't have to wait long for a table.
Via Baccina 42, tel. 06-4883198, al42.it, open Mon & Wed-Sun 12:30-3:30pm & 7-9:30pm, €10, Metro B, B1 Cavour, Tram 8 Venezia

22 You can find Neapolitan street food in the heart of Rome at **Ce Stamo a Pensà.** This is a little hole in the wall, so get your order to go—among your choices are pizza fritta (fried pizza), panino, and parmigiana di melanzane (eggplant parmesan)—and eat it on the steps of the fountain in Piazza della Madonna dei Monti.
Via Leonina 81, tel. 06-69363154, open Mon-Thu 9-1:30am, Fri 9-2am, Sat 10-2am, Sun 9-1am, aperitivo €5, montanara €4, Metro B, B1 Cavour, Tram 8 Venezia

27 With so many gelato flavors to choose from, you might feel the pressure of FOMO, so you'll want to head to **Gelateria S.M. Maggiore,** which is popular for its unique concoctions. Ever tasted fig or apple quince gelato? For visitors with dietary restrictions, there are gluten-free, lactose-free, and vegan choices.
Via Cavour 93a/95, tel. 06-39366976, open daily noon-midnight, gelato €3.80, Metro B, B1 Cavour

29 **Blackmarket Hall** has the vibes and looks of a speakeasy from the 1920s. Dark antique furniture, dark red walls, romantic lighting, velvet curtains, and vintage decoration on the walls. The tastiest cocktails are here, along with the most flavorful food and fine music.
Via de' Ciancaleoni 31, tel. 349-199-5295, blackmarkethall.com, open Mon-Sat 6pm-2am, Sun 6pm-1am, cocktail €14, Metro B, B1 Cavour, Tram 5, 14 Farini

31 Romans have been quenching their thirst for wine at **Ai Tre Scalini** since 1895, and it is still just as popular today. Choose one of their great wines and order something regional to snack on, such as cicoria or porchetta.
Via Panisperna 251, tel. 06-48907495, aitrescalini.org, open daily 12:30pm-1am, glass of wine €6, Metro B, B1 Cavour, Tram 8 Venezia

34
Enoteca

22
SACCOCCIA

31

35

34 **Al Vino Al Vino** is a low-lit wine bar that can get warm and crowded, but the vibe is always good. The wine menu is impressive while the food menu is concise, but for a few euros you can order a small plate with fresh zucchini, dried tomatoes, and homemade caponata (stewed eggplant).
Via dei Serpenti 19, tel. 06-485803, open daily 10am-2pm& 6pm-midnight, glass wine €5, Metro B, B1 Cavour, Tram 8 Venezia

35 In a small, ivy-covered house you'll find aperitivo and cocktail bar **La Casetta a Monti.** The signature cocktails are unique and intriguing, such as the Bee's Knees—a gin-based cocktail with lime and honey. In addition to the regular cocktails, new ones are invented every week, and you can enjoy until late in the evening.
Via della Madonna dei Monti 62, tel. 333-584-4561, la-casetta-a-monti.webnode.it, open daily 6pm-2am, cocktail € 12, Metro B, B1 Cavour, Tram 8 Venezia

36 Don't let the small, unassuming entrance of this pizzeria fool you. At the back of **Pizzeria alle Carrette** is a huge outdoor terrace. This is the go-to place when you fancy a typical Roman pizza that is thin, crispy, and richly topped.
Via della Madonna dei Monti 95, tel. 06-6792770, open daily noon-3:30pm & 6:45-11:30pm, pizza €9, Metro B, B1 Cavour, Tram 8 Venezia

37 The owners of **La Taverna dei Fori Imperiali** pride themselves on having fed famous stars such as Dustin Hoffman and Al Pacino; the walls are full of photos as proof. And no wonder—it's a nice place to be, and it's loved by many. The gnocchi al tartufo is delicious. Reservations are in order!
Via della Madonna dei Monti 9, tel. 06-6798643, open Mon & Wed-Sun 12:30-3pm & 7:30-10:30pm, €18, Metro B, B1 Cavour, Tram 8 Venezia

SHOPPING

4 The best way to describe **Pasticceria Cipriani** is that it's an old-fashioned Italian cookie store. The bakery was founded in 1906 by Pietro Cipriani, and it is now managed by the fourth generation of the Cipriani family. The original

recipes of the family business are still used today to bake all the cookies, cakes, and pies.

Via Carlo Botta 21/23, pasticceriacipriani.com, open Tue-Sat 10am-1:30pm & 4-7:30pm, Metro Vittorio Emanuele, Tram 5, 14 Vittorio Emanuele

23 If you're searching for a leather bag or accessory, look inside **Hang Roma.** The designs are cool, sleek, and practical, yet they have a vintage look and feel. All items are handmade in Italy from the finest leather.

Via degli Zingari 32, hangroma.it, open Mon-Sat 10:30am-7:30pm, Metro B, B1 Cavour, Tram 5, 14 Farini

25 At concept store **LOL** you can find beautiful, sustainable garments of high quality. In addition to their own line, they sell items from small European designers, such as linen dresses, silk blouses, knitted sweaters, funky jewelry, and fantastic shoes.

Via Urbana 92, lolroma.myshopify.com, open daily 11am-2pm & 3-8pm, Metro B, B1 Cavour, Tram 5, 14 Farini

26 Not only is the green façade of **Elena Kihlman Design** beautiful to look at, but all the goodies inside are fun too. Owner Elena designs textiles for home and fashion accessories. And in addition to her creations, you can also find products by other designers. There is unique dinnerware, clocks with crazy prints, and colorful trays.

Via Urbana 101, elenakihlman.com, open Mon-Sat 10am-8pm, Sun 11am-8pm, Metro B, B1 Cavour

30 Flowery prints and stripes, dresses, and shirts—at **Kokoro** you're guaranteed to find the perfect piece. When a customer enters the store, needles and threads are temporarily put on hold. None of the items cost more than €70, yet everything is of very high quality.

Via del Boschetto 75, kokoroshop.it, open daily 11am-8pm, Metro B, B1 Cavour, Tram 5, 14 Farini

33

30

23

LABORATORIO

32 Although the straightforward name belies the whimsy of the products, **Candle Store** has been creating unique, artistic candles with elegant and luxurious designs since 1997. The collection features the delightful, iconic designs they call La Ciotola (the bowl), all'Uovo (the egg), and al Bicchiere (the glass).
Via dei Serpenti 127, candlestore.it, open Mon 3-8pm, Tue-Sat 10am-8pm, Metro B, B1 Cavour, Tram 8 Venezia

33 **Pifebo Vintage Shop** has it all: great Adidas track suits, quality leather jackets, and well-priced bags. You can also find nice shirts and shoes, as well as their own line of sunglasses, which are new but look vintage.
Via dei Serpenti 135/136, pifebo.com, open Mon-Sat 11am-8pm, Sun noon-8pm, Metro B, B1 Cavour, Tram 8 Venezia

MORE TO EXPLORE

5 The **Parco del Colle Oppio** on Oppio Hill (not one of Rome's seven hills), under which Emperor Nero's golden house is buried, has perhaps the most extraordinary view of any park in Rome. It's especially beautiful at the beginning and end of the day when the light falls very nicely on the Colosseum.
Viale del Monte Oppio, open daily 6:30am-9pm, free, Metro B, B1 Colosseo, Tram 3, 8 Piazza del Colosseo

19 In ancient Rome, next to the Fori Imperiali, was the working-class neighborhood of Suburra: it was crowded with tall buildings, and fires broke out every so often. The thick, fireproof wall between the Fori and Suburra was, therefore, a critical layer of protection. But because the Fori had such an important public function, accessibility was also a requirement. The **Arco dei Pantani** is the passageway between the two areas.
Via Tor de' Conti, Metro B, B1 Cavour, Tram 8 Venezia

21 The heart of Monti belongs to the Madonna. The little square **Piazza della Madonna dei Monti** is named after the adjacent church (the Santa Maria ai Monti), and it is always vibrant and cozy. In terms of terraces, you have plenty to choose from here, but you can also take a seat by the fountain.
Piazza della Madonna dei Monti, Metro B, B1 Cavour, Tram 8 Venezia

24 **Antigallery** takes a somewhat more relaxed approach to gallery work. Here, you can enjoy art while also enjoying a beer. Don't forget to explore the terrace and the gallery's surroundings as well. The Antigallery is located on a delightful little square.
Piazza degli Zingari 3, open daily 5pm-2am, free, Metro B, B1 Cavour, Tram 5, 14 Farini

WALK 3

PANTHEON, GHETTO & AVENTINO

ABOUT THE WALK

This walk takes you through downtown from north to south. You'll start in the heart of the Centro Storico at the Pantheon and find your way to Circo Massimo (Circus Maximus) and Aventino (Aventine Hill) through the heart of the Ghetto, Tiber Island, and a quiet stretch of Trastevere.

THE NEIGHBORHOODS

You cannot miss the **Pantheon** on your visit to Rome. It was built at the start of the 2nd century CE and has witnessed everything. It's an incredible building that will undoubtedly make a lasting impression.

The Colonna di Marco Aurelio is nearly 100 feet high (30 m) and wrapped with gorgeous reliefs. The Baroque Jesuit churches of Sant'Ignazio and Il Gesù vie for Rome's most impressive ceilings (not counting those in Vatican City). The temples on the Area Sacra dell'Argentina were built during the time of the Roman Republic. What was at the time the site of the Senate building and where Julius Caesar was assassinated has slowly grown into a gathering place for the cats of Rome.

This route then passes through the Roman Jewish ghetto that houses the oldest Jewish community in Europe. The first Jews settled in Rome as early as the time of the Roman Republic, across the Tiber in Trastevere. Around 1200, the community moved to the present-day **Ghetto di Roma**. In 1555 Pope Paul IV determined that the Jewish community in the papal state should live in an isolated zone, which had to be walled in, following the Venetian example. The wall was demolished in 1888. During this time, a unique Roman-Jewish cuisine emerged there, and many of the dishes are still popular today.

This walk traverses the little island in the Tiber, sneaks a bit through **Trastevere** and past the ancient Roman cattle market Foro Boario and the Bocca della Verità, and arrives at the **Circo Massimo.** Domitian had a new palace built on Palatino that overlooked the circus. From here there is another great view of the remains of the palace, along with an even more spectacular view of it from the Roseto Comunale. The climb up **Aventino** is rewarded with two very nice views.

SHORT ON TIME? HERE ARE THE HIGHLIGHTS:

1 COLONNA DI MARCO AURELIO + 6 PANTHEON + 22 TEMPIO MAGGIORE/MUSEO EBRAICO DI ROMA + 32 CIRCO MASSIMO + 34 GIARDINO DEGLI ARANCI

TIPS

// A fun walk for those who have visited Rome before // Giardino degli Aranci is a great place to see the sunset // Your walk (and climb) will be rewarded with delicious food!

PANTHEON, GHETTO & AVENTINO

1. **Colonna di Marco Aurelio**
2. 9Hotel Cesàri & Terrazza
3. Salotto42
4. Venchi
5. Armando al Pantheon
6. **Pantheon**
7. Piazza della Minerva
8. Sant'Ignazio di Loyola
9. Palazzo Doria Pamphilj/ Galleria Doria Pamphilj
10. Palazzo Bonaparte
11. ViVi Bistrot
12. Ristorante Plebiscito
13. Chiesa del Gesù
14. Fox Gallery
15. Area Sacra dell'Argentina
16. Fontana delle Tartarughe
17. Il Museo del Louvre
18. Su'Ghetto
19. Pasticceria Boccione
20. Beppe e i Suoi Formaggi
21. Open Baladin
22. **Tempio Maggiore/Museo Ebraico di Roma**
23. Teatro di Marcello
24. Isola Tiberina
25. Trattoria da Enzo al 29
26. L'Ora del Te
27. 404 Name Not Found
28. Foro Boario
29. Bocca della Verità/Santa Maria in Cosmedin
30. Mercato di Campagna Amica
31. Circoletto
32. **Circo Massimo**
33. Roseto Comunale
34. **Giardino degli Aranci**
35. Piazza dei Cavalieri di Malta
36. Tram Depot
37. Felice a Testaccio
38. Lo Scopettaro

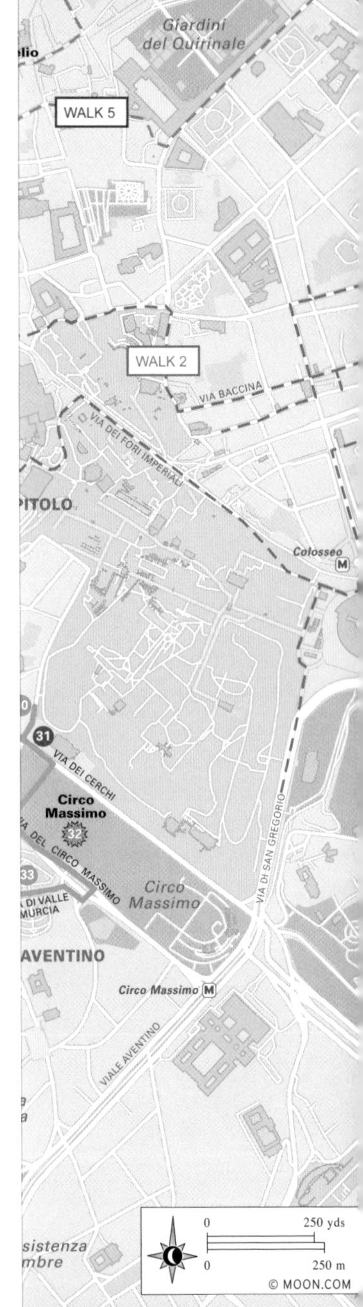

WALK 3 DESCRIPTION (approx. 5 mi/8 km)

Start at the Column of Marcus Aurelius 1 and turn left onto Via dei Bergamaschi to Piazza di Pietra for a cappuccino with a view 2 or wine 3. Leave the square on the right and follow Via dei Pastini for the best gelato 4. Walk across Piazza della Rotonda and stop at Salita de' Crescenzi for old-school food 5 before visiting the impressive Pantheon 6. Walk behind the Pantheon to Piazza della Minerva 7. Proceed on Via Santa Caterina da Siena and turn left onto Via di Sant'Ignazio, toward the church 8. Turn right as you exit the church and right on Via del Corso to visit a private art collection 9. Continue on Via del Corso and visit the home of Napoleon's mother 10. After all the splendor, it's time for a light lunch 11 or a traditional pasta on Via del Plebiscito 12. Continue past the mother church of the Jesuits on the left 13 and souvenirs on the right 14. When you see excavations 15, cross Via Florida and walk across into the Ghetto at Piazza Mattei 16. Continue down Via delle Reginella, past the photographs 17, to Via del Portico d'Ottavia. Turn right for a typical Roman-Jewish meal 18 with a delicious cake for dessert 19. Walk up Via di Santa Maria del Pianto for tasty cheeses 20. Walk a bit farther, turning right around the little park and right again on Via degli Specchi for a cold beer 21. Walk back and turn right on Via Arenula and left on Lungotevere de' Cenci to reach the Jewish synagogue and museum 22. Behind the synogogue, find a footpath to the Teatro di Marcello 23, then walk back and cross the Tiber to the little island 24. Walk over the next bridge and turn left, turn right on Via Titta Scarpetta, then left on Via dei Salumi for delicious food 25, and right again for special tea service 26. Or turn right for a terrace 27. Turn left on Via Augusto Jandolo, left again on Via Pietro Peretti, and take the Palatino bridge to Foro Boario 28 and reenact the famous scene from *Roman Holiday* 29. Turn right toward the square, turn right on Via del Cerchi, and left at the intersection for snacks 30. Walk back a bit, order a cold drink 31, and imagine yourself in *Ben Hur* 32. Walk across the old racetrack and follow the road with Circo Massimo on your left. Cross the road to the Rose Garden 33 then climb Aventino to enter the Orange Garden 34 where the view is even more spectacular. Peek through the keyhole 35 and go back down Via di Porta Lavernale. Relax on the terrace by the streetcar 36 then go for a good bowl of pasta 37. Continue north on Via Mastro Giorgo and cross Piazza di S. Maria Liberatrice. On Lungotevere Testaccio, you will find the perfect restaurant to end the day 38.

SIGHTS & ATTRACTIONS

1 Standing almost 100 feet tall (30 m), the **Colonna di Marco Aurelio** is in the middle of the Piazza Colonna. The picture relief that winds around the column recounts the events in wars waged by this Roman emperor in the 2nd century—even the brutal ones. Since the end of the 16th century, a statue of the apostle Paul, one of the patron saints of Rome, has stood atop the column instead of a depiction of the emperor.

Piazza Colonna, Metro Barberini, Tram 8 Venezia

6 The **Pantheon** stands on the site where Marcus Agrippa (the righthand man to Emperor Augustus) had a temple built in 27-25 BCE. A fire destroyed this original temple, and when the current Pantheon was consecrated in 126 CE, the inscription on the façade crediting Marcus's work was retained: M.AGRIPPA.L.F.COS.TERTIVM.FECIT (made by M. Agrippa, son of Lucius, consul for the third time). This edifice has seen some nineteen hundred years of history, and its dome contains an oculus that allows a beam of light to dramatically shine into the dim interior.

Piazza della Rotonda, pantheonroma.com, open Mon-Sat 9am-7pm (ticket office until 6pm), €5, Metro Abarberini, Tram 8 Venezia

7 The little elephant in **Piazza della Minerva** is not the work Bernini was most proud of. Pope Alexander VII feared the marble statue could not support the heavy Egyptian obelisk, so he ordered the elephant's legs to be shortened. Bernini still tried to hide this by dressing up the little elephant somewhat, but the result is still not the stately symbol of wisdom he had in mind. The Romans mockingly call the elephant "il porcellino," Italian for "little piggy." But il porcellino soon became pulcino in the Roman dialect—hence, you are now looking at Bernini's "little chick."

Piazza della Minerva 42, Metro Barberini, Tram 8 Venezia

8 Come to **Sant'Ignazio di Loyola** church to see Andrea Pozzo's magnificent ceiling fresco, which depicts Ignatius of Loyola, founding father of the Society of Jesus (Jesuit order), surrounded by angels while soaring to up to heaven. Because the Jesuits decorated the interior with an abundance of frescos, gold

1

8

leaf, and marble, they didn't have any money left to construct a dome. Andrea Pozzo solved this problem by painting a striking illusion of a dome.
Via del Caravita 8a, santignazio.gesuiti.it, open daily 9am-8pm, free, Metro Barberini, Tram 8 Venezia

9 Since the 17th century the spacious **Palazzo Doria Pamphilj** has been home to the descendants of this wealthy aristocratic family. Inside is the **Galleria Doria Pamphilj,** with one of the most important private art collections in Italy, including masterpieces by Italian artists such as Bernini, Raphael, and Caravaggio, as well as works by Jan van Scorel, Pieter Bruegelteh Elder, and his son Jan Bruegel the Elder. The audio tour even features the voice of a living family member—a prince, no less.
Via del Corso 305, doriapamphilj.it, open Mon-Thu 9am-7pm, Fri-Sun 10am-8pm, museum €16, Metro Barberini, Tram 8 Venezia

10 **Palazzo Bonaparte** is named after Letizia Bonaparte, mother of Napoleon and owner of the building from 1818 to 1836. The palace is best known for its striking green balcony. According to legend, until her death, Letizia kept a close eye on all comings and goings, both in Piazza Venezia and Via del Corso, through the crevices of the porch. The doors of the historic palace are now open to anyone who wants to enjoy the same view. There are exhibitions you can visit as well.
Piazza Venezia 5, mostrepalazzobonaparte.it, open daily Jul-Aug 11am-9pm, Sep-Jun 10am-8pm, €16, Tram 8 Venezia

13 The **Chiesa del Gesù** was built between 1568 and 1584. It was a thank you gift from Cardinal Farnese to the Society of Jesus for its struggle during the Counter-Reformation. The Renaissance had peaked, and the Jesuit style is considered the transition to the Baroque period. Baciccio's impressive ceiling fresco is the pinnacle: it's busy, full, rich, and dynamic. In "Triumph in the Name of Jesus," they mercilessly hurl heretics and pagans out of heaven.
Piazza del Gesù, chiesadelgesu.org, open daily 7:30am-12:30pm & 4-7:30pm, free, Tram 8 Venezia

15 The temples of **Area Sacra dell'Argentina** date to the Roman Republic and are among the oldest in Rome. Some archaeologists believe this is the original site of the Curia of Pompey—the Senate building where Julius Caesar was assassinated. In 2023, the Area rolled out renovations that include a self-guided walking route with interpretive signs that take people through the artifacts and excavations. There is also a cat shelter here.

Via di San Nicola de' Cesarini 10, open last Sun Mar-last Sat Oct Tue-Sun 9:30am-7pm, last Sun Oct-last Sat Mar Tue-Sun 9:30am-4pm, €5, Tram 8 Arenula/Cairoli

16 On the elegant Piazza Mattei you'll find the beautiful **Fontana delle Tartarughe** (turtle fountain). The story goes that a man had this fountain built overnight to impress the father of the woman he wished to marry. The original plan included dolphins spouting water, but the water pressure was too low, so turtles were depicted instead.

Piazza Mattei, Tram 8 Arenula/Cairoli

22 The **Tempio Maggiore** and the **Museo Ebraico di Roma** form the heart of the Jewish Quarter, and it's where you will find the oldest Jewish community in Europe. The first Jews came there as early as the time of the Roman Republic, and initially they settled across the Tiber River. Around 1200 the community moved to the present Ghetto di Roma. In 1555 Pope Paul IV decreed the community should live in an isolated zone where the gates would be closed between sunset and sunrise. Until 1870, Roman Jews were required to live in the Ghetto. The wall was demolished in 1888.

Lungotevere de' Cenci, romaebraica.it, synagogue open Mon-Thu & Sun 10am-5pm, Fri 9am-2pm museum Tue-Thu 10am-5:15pm, Fri 9am-3:15pm, synagogue + museum €11, Tram 8 Arenula (Ministero Giustizia)

23 Julius Caesar initiated the construction of the **Teatro di Marcello** (Theater of Marcellus), one of the largest theaters in ancient Rome, and Augustus finished it around 12 BCE. Augustus dedicated the theater to his nephew Marcellus. Houses were later built on top of the theater, and a few lucky Romans still live in them today.

Via del Teatro di Marcello, open daily summer 9am-7pm, winter 9am-6pm, free, Tram 8 Arenula/Cairoli

28 There are two temples left on the **Foro Boario**—the ancient cattle market. They date to the first and second centuries BCE and have been very well maintained because they were used as churches in later years. The round temple was dedicated to Hercules Victor, and the square one—a typical Roman design with a covered entrance at the front—was dedicated to Portunus, the god of ports and harbors. The forum was an important trade market, as one of the main ports of the Tiber River used to be nearby.
Piazza della Bocca della Verità, Tram 8 Belli

29 Do not attempt to visit this site unless you have a clear conscience, because rumor has it that the **Bocca della Verità** (Mouth of Truth) will bite off the hand of any liar. According to local legend, a magician who wanted to test the virtue of married women cast a spell on this statue. It was featured in the Gregory Peck and Audrey Hepburn movie, *Roman Holiday.* When you visit, be sure to stop in the neighboring church. **Santa Maria in Cosmedin** is famous for its 12th century floors, frescos, and the shards of mosaic in the sacristy.
Piazza della Bocca della Verità 18, turismoroma.it/it/luoghi/bocca-della-verita, church open daily summer 9:30am-1pm, 2-6pm, winter 9:30am-1m, 2-5pm, free, Tram 8 Belli

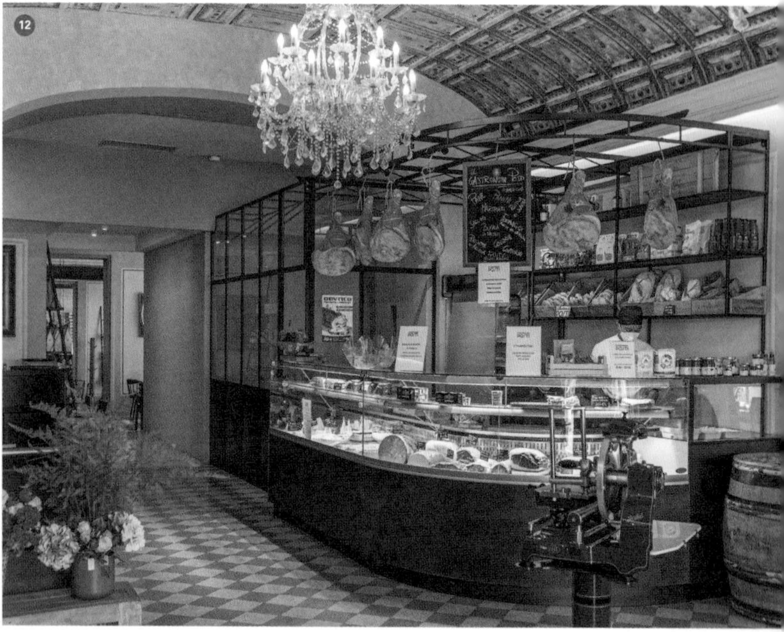
12

21
open
baladin
ROMA

21
Baladin
OPEN

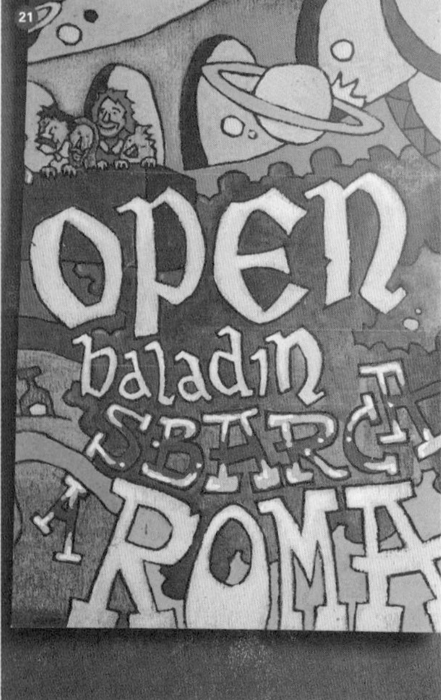

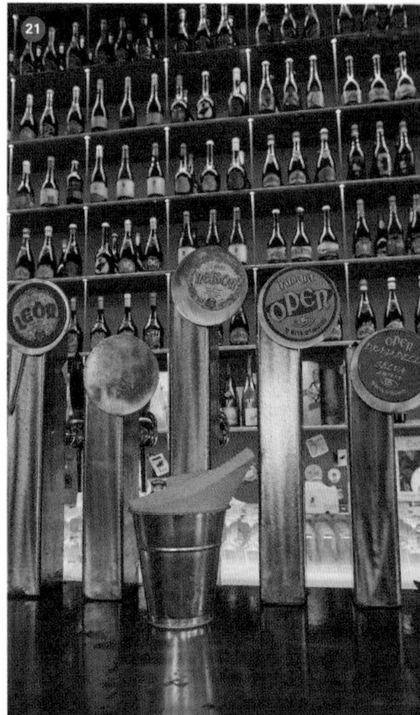

32 You will need to use your imagination when looking at the grounds that once were **Circo Massimo.** This is where the emperors of Rome organized chariot races that were often frequented by some three hundred thousand spectators. The imperial grandstand, where the emperor and his family watched the spectacle, was connected to the palace on Palatino. Today, Circo Massimo has a different vibe—although it still hosts sporting events, it's also a park where people lounge and relax, and it's used for concerts and staged battles.
Via del Circo Massimo, Metro B, B1 Circo Massimo, Tram 3, 8 Aventino/Circo Massimo

FOOD & DRINK

2 The beautiful rooftop patio of **9Hotel Cesàri & Terrazza** is an ideal place to relax, especially on warmer days. It's situated in the heart of Rome and has very comfortable seating, plants, and the Church of Sant'Ignazio di Loyola as a backdrop. It's the perfect place for a cup of coffee, an ice-cold glass of wine, and pinsa for lunch.
Via di Pietra 89/a, tel. 06-6749701, 9-hotel-cesari-rome.it, open daily noon-midnight, cocktail €16, Metro Barberini, Tram 8 Venezia

3 At this prominent spot in central Rome, next to Hadrian's Temple, is the trendy cocktail bar **Salotto42.** The seating inside is limited, but there is a fantastic outdoor patio. Enjoy a long, relaxing dinner overlooking a beautiful set of historic columns. On summer evenings you'll be in the front row for a free light show called "Luci sul Tempio di Adriano."
Piazza di Pietra 42, tel. 06-6785804, salotto42.it, open daily 10:30-2am, cocktail €12, lunch €15, Metro Barberini, Tram 8 Venezia

4 **Venchi** might be crowded by tourists, and it has several establishments in the city, but it is also rightly known as one of the best gelato parlors in Rome. The establishment near the Trevi Fountain has a chocolate waterfall. The gelato is homemade, and the chocolate is made onsite, but that usually goes without saying in Rome.
Via degli Orfani 87, tel. 06-69925423, it.venchi.com, open daily 11am-9:30pm, gelato €3.60, Metro Barberini, Tram 8 Venezia

5 Cork wall tiles, a stained-glass door, and a menu that has remained the same for decades—**Armando al Pantheon** is an institution for old-school Roman dining at its best. The menu features many classic pasta dishes, as well as specialties such as guinea fowl with porcini mushrooms. It's a busy restaurant in a well-trafficked location, so reservations are recommended.
Salita dei Crescenzi 31, tel. 06-68803034, armandoalpantheon.it, open daily 12:30-3pm & 7-11pm, €18, Metro Barberini, Tram 8 Venezia

11 **ViVi Bistrot** is in the royal halls of Palazzo Bonaparte. Vivi's style is eclectic mixed with classic—royal blue on one wall, modern pink on another. This is the place for classic Italian dishes, as well as pinsas, (vegan and beef) burgers, smoothies, and salads.
Piazza Venezia 5, tel. 06-69228769, vivi.it, open daily 9am-9pm, €15, Tram 8 Venezia

12 **Ristorante Plebiscito** caters to all tastes. There are delicacies in the small mercato, such as bottles of wine, cold cuts, and local cheeses. It has cozy and hearty atmosphere and is attractively decorated with retro floor tiles, a Roman ceiling, and antique wooden furniture.
Via del Plebiscito 104, tel. 06-6785440, plebiscito.net, open daily 7am-midnight, €17, Tram 8 Venezia

18 During the years of when Roman Jews were forced to live in the Ghetto, isolated from the rest of Rome, a unique Roman-Jewish cuisine emerged, and many of the dishes are still popular today. **Su'Ghetto** restaurant features traditional Jewish food, which means all dishes are kosher and dairy-free. Try the carciofi alla giudia (deep-fried artichokes).
Via del Portico d'Ottavia 1c, telephone 06-68805605, sughetto.it, open Mon-Thu & Sun noon-11pm, Fri noon-3pm, Sat 6-11pm, €19, Tram 8 Arenula/Cairoli

21 More and more small breweries are opening in Rome, all with craft beers. **Open Baladin** has more than 140 varieties on the menu with about 40 on tap, and it serves homemade potato chips and hamburgers.
Via degli Specchi 6, tel. 06-6838989, openbaladinroma.it, open Mon-Thu & Sun noon-1am, Fri-Sat noon-2pm, beer €5, Tram 8 Arenula/Cairoli

25 **Trattoria da Enzo al 29** has Roman classics such as amatriciana, gricia, cacio e pepe, and carbonara. It's a small, simple, atmospheric, and simply good place to have a hearty meal. It's located in a quieter part of Trastevere, near the Tiber, and the restaurant is a classic in the neighborhood.

Via dei Vascellari 29, tel. 06-5812260, daenzoal29.com, open Mon-Sat 12:15-3pm & 7-11pm, €14.50, Tram 8 Belli

27 In a quieter part of Trastevere, the terrace of **404 Name Not Found** is the ideal place to take a break. The menu offers something for every moment of the day: a good cappuccino with cornetto in the morning, a three-course meal, a tasty sandwich for lunch, and a great aperitivo at the end of the day.

Via dei Genovesi 1, tel. 327-094-8005, open Tue-Thu & Sun 6:30am-11pm, Fri-Sat 6:30-1am, €11, Tram 8 Trastevere (Mastai)

31 Near the Circo Massimo is the cool and funky restaurant **Circoletto.** This is the place for the no-nonsense people of Rome. There is an extensive beer

25

25

selection, natural wines, skateboards on the wall, and the occasional DJ in the corner. Here, many drinks are served ice cold, the music is good, and the comfort food is shared. Feel free to order your beer as a take-away and have a seat on the walls of Circo Massimo.

Via dei Cerchi 55, tel. 06-83777691, open Mon-Sat 6pm-midnight, €7, Metro B, B1 Circo Massimo, Tram 3, 8 Aventino/Circo Massimo

36 In working-class Testaccio, you'll find one of the city's most unique terraces at **Tram Depot.** Neighbors drop by at the converted streetcar for a quick coffee at the bar. Order a caffè, spremuta, or spritz, and take a seat under the trees.

Via Marmorata 13, open Mon-Sat 8-2am, Sun 8am-midnight, coffee €1, Metro B, B1 Piramide, Tram 3, 8 Marmorata/Galvani

37 Every day the chef at **Felice a Testaccio** serves a different traditional dish, such as tortellini on Mondays and fish on Fridays (of course). The menu features daily specials, but mainstays such as involtini in sugo (beef rolls) are popular favorites at this busy restaurant.

Via Mastro Giorgio 29, tel. 06-5746800, feliceatestaccio.it, open daily 12:30-3:30pm & 7-11:30pm, pasta €14, Metro B, B1 Piramide, Tram 3, 8 Marmorata/Galvani

38 **Lo Scopettaro** is one of the oldest trattorias in Rome and has been serving traditional dishes for more than eighty years. Roman cuisine is known for its simplicity, born as a poor peasant's cuisine that used ingredients that would otherwise be left over, such as oxtail, pork cheek, and organ meat. Try the antipasto tipico Romano with coratella (intestines of small animals), trippa (tripe), and fagioli al coccio (baked beans). Don't worry, they also have more modern dishes on the menu.

Lungotevere Testaccio 7, tel. 06-5757912, loscopettaroroma.com, open daily 12:30-2:45pm & 7:30-10:45pm, €15, Tram 8 Emporio

SHOPPING

14 The people at **Fox Gallery,** who are always friendly, sell posters, postcards, notebooks, and small paintings. The assortment is extensive, so it's worth checking whether they have something that calls your name. Fun and practical souvenirs can be bought here in the form of a journal with a beautiful image of Rome on the cover.
Corso Vittorio Emanuele II 5, fox-gallery.scontrinoshop.com, open daily 11am-2:30pm & 3:30-7pm, Tram 8 Venezia

17 **Il Museo del Louvre** has a collection of about thirty thousand intriguing vintage photographs. Some are by well-known photographers or agencies, but in most cases the photographer of the family snapshots, cityscapes, and fashion shoots remains forever anonymous.
Via della Reginella 8a, ilmuseodellouvre.com, open Mon-Sat 11am-2pm & 2:30-7pm, free, Tram 8 Arenula/Cairoli

19 For six generations, the Limentani family has run the kosher family bakery **Pasticceria Boccione.** They have the most delicious amaretti (ginger cookies) and cocoa biscotti (chocolate cookies), but you can't leave here without also tasting the traditional torta ricotta e visciole (cake with ricotta and sour cherries).
Via del Portico d'Ottavia 1, open Jan-Jul & Sep-Dec Mon-Thu 7am-7pm, Fri 7am-4pm, Sun 7am-6pm, Tram 8 Arenula/Cairoli

20 The display cases at **Beppe e i Suoi Formaggi** ("Beppe and his cheeses") are filled to the brim with dozens of cheeses, while in the back of the store whole cheeses mature in a glass climate chamber. Purchase some exciting cheeses for a picnic or sit down in the shop itself for a cheese tasting with accompanying wines.
Via Santa Maria del Pianto 9a, open Mon-Sat 11am-11:30pm, Tram 8 Arenula/Cairoli

26 Italy and Rome are not known for tea, but **L'Ora del Te** might change how you feel about that. This is paradise for lovers of vintage and design, combined

20
Beppe

26

14
I WOULD RATHER BE AT HOGWARTS
OH!
RUGGINE
ZEROCALCARE

20
Beppe
E I SUOI FORMAGGI

with a bit of humor. Everything in the store is there for a reason. You can also buy extraordinary tableware and elegant accessories for the home.

Via dei Vascellari 25, open Mon 3:30-7:30pm, Tue-Sat 10:30am-2pm & 3:30-7:30pm, Tram 8 Belli

MORE TO EXPLORE

24 In summer, the banks of the Tiber River and those of the **Isola Tiberina** are filled with stalls and cafés. The Fatebenefratelli Hospital on the island operates year-round. The Ponte Fabricio is the only Old Roman bridge still completely intact: it dates to 62 BCE. Ristorante Tiberino is a good place for lunch.

Isola Tiberina, Tram 8 Belli

30 Every weekend local artisans and farmers flock to the city to sell their wares at markets such as **Mercato di Campagna Amica.** Here you can see, sample, and shop for fresh fruits and vegetables, wines and oils, dairy products, sausages, and hams. At the back of the hall is a small outdoor patio where you can have a quick lunch.
Via di San Teodoro 74, campagnamica.it, open Sat-Sun 8am-3pm, Tram 8 Belli

33 The **Roseto Comunale** rose gardens are located on a site that used to be a Jewish cemetery. This is commemorated by the paths and plantings that (from above) form the shape of a seven-branched Menorah, the candelabrum. Visit in May and June when the flowers are in bloom and the gardens are open to the public. It's a nice place for a breezy walk and a phenomenal view of Palatino and the city.
Via di Valle Murcia 6, turismoroma.it/it/luoghi/roseto-comunale, open daily mid Apr-mid Jun 8:30am-7:30pm, free, Metro B, B1 Circo Massimo, Tram 3, 8 Aventino/Circo Massimo

34 The **Giardino degli Aranci** was built within the medieval walls of an ancient fortress. It's one of the prettiest places in the city. From the garden with orange trees, you have a magnificent view of the Basilica di San Pietro and the city center.
Piazza Pietro d'Illiria, open daily sunrise to sunset, free, Metro B, B1 Circo Massimo, Tram 3, 8 Emporio

35 The keyhole of the Cavalieri di Malta was made famous by the movie *La Grande Bellezza*. Therefore, in **Piazza dei Cavalieri di Malta** there is always a line of tourists, all wanting to peer through the keyhole. Just get in line; the view will surprise you. The monastery church belongs to the Knights of the Maltese Order, which used to organize crusades. The Order has its sovereign state here with its own head of state, passports, and license plates.
Piazza dei Cavalieri di Malta 4, Tram 3, 8 Marmorata/Galvani

WALK 4

VATICANO, BORGO & PRATI

ABOUT THE WALK

The Vatican City is modest in size, but in terms of art and architecture, it is enormous. In the Musei Vaticani you can walk for miles without realizing it. The imposing St. Peter's Basilica is the largest church in the world. Bernini designed an equally impressive square in front of the church. And in the nearby neighborhood of Prati, you can enjoy an afternoon of walking, shopping, and imbibing.

THE NEIGHBORHOODS

Vaticano (the **Vatican**) is an autonomous state in the middle of Rome and is worth a dedicated day or two to see its main sights: the Musei Vaticani (Vatican Museums) and St. Peter's Basilica (Basilica di San Pietro). Plan ahead and know what you want to see because these sights can be overwhelming.

The Musei Vaticani contains two masterpieces that were created simultaneously. Raphael and his many assistants painted the frescoes in the papal apartments of Julius II (known today as the Raphael Rooms), while at the same time Michelangelo toiled at the frescoes on the ceiling of the Sistine Chapel. A sculptor, Michelangelo had never painted a fresco before, which makes the resulting masterpiece even more remarkable. Try to get a table at a restaurant at the nearby **Piazza del Risorgimento** and recharge before you visit St. Peter's Basilica. From the moment you enter **Piazza San Pietro** (St. Peter's Square) you will go from one amazement to another, if only for the grandeur of it all.

The **Via della Conciliazione** in the medieval **Borgo** neighborhood was built by Mussolini to celebrate the Lateran Treaty: the treaty in which Italy and the Vatican City agreed on the status quo that is still active today. To the left of Via della Conciliazione you can turn into Borgo and enter another world.

End your day filled with art and culture in **Prati.** The area where Prati (fields) is located still consisted of vineyards, pastures, and some farms until well into the 19th century. The neighborhood was created so the bourgeoisie could have space. Because the relationship between Italy and the Vatican at that time was still very tense, the street plan was designed in a way that the dome of the Basilica was virtually invisible. Today wealthy Romans still live here, and it's a place where you come for shopping, eating, drinking, and entertainment.

SHORT ON TIME? HERE ARE THE HIGHLIGHTS:
7 RAPHAEL'S ROOMS + 8 SISTINE CHAPEL +
14 ST. PETER'S BASILICA + 15 CUPOLA OF ST. PETER'S +
25 COLA DI RIENZO

VATICANO, BORGO & PRATI

1 Trecaffè
2 Re-Bio
3 Musei Vaticani
4 Cortile della Pigna
5 Galleria degli Arazzi
6 Galleria delle Carte Geografiche
7 **Raphael Rooms**
8 **Sistine Chapel**
9 Scala Elicoidale Momo
10 Giardini Vaticani
11 200°
12 La Zanzara
13 Piazza San Pietro
14 **St. Peter's Basilica**
15 **Cupola of St. Peter's**
16 Borgosteria
17 Borghiciana Pastificio Artigianale
18 Terrazza Les Étoiles
19 Emerald's Independent Bar
20 Pompi
21 Port à Demìe
22 Callipo
23 Guttilla Alta Gelateria Italiana
24 Castroni
25 **Coin Excelsior/Cola di Rienzo**
26 Il Gianfornaio
27 Chopstick
28 BallereTTe
29 Bialetti Home
30 Iron G Superstore
31 Kozmo Laze
32 Piazza Cavour
33 Corte Suprema di Cassazione
34 Salvatore
35 Ponte Umberto I
36 Bibliobar
37 Castel Sant'Angelo
38 Ponte Sant'Angelo

WALK 4 DESCRIPTION (approx. 4 mi/7 km)

Start with a coffee 1 or go left up Via Germanico for a vitamin shot 2. Walk back slightly to the walls of the Vatican. Brave the Vatican Museums and the incredibly large, beautiful, lavish collection 3. Be sure to see Bramante's Cortile della Pigna 4. Experience the Mona Lisa effect in the Galleria degli Arazzi 5. Marvel at the maps in the Galleria delle Carte Geografiche 6. Feast your eyes in the Raphael Rooms 7 and let the Sistine Chapel 8 take your breath away. Leave the museum via the Scala Elicoidale Momo 9 or have a guided tour in the gardens 10. Walk back, turn right around the walls and left at the curve to recover with a sandwich 11, or keep walking around Piazza del Risorgimento and through Via Crescenzio for a sumptuous lunch 12. Walk back to the square and turn left on Via del Mascherino to be overwhelmed by St. Peter's Square 13. Admire Michelangelo's *Pietà* 14 and climb the dome 15. Walk a bit on Via della Conciliazione and then turn left on Via dell'Erba, then turn left on Borgo Pio for the finest osteria in the area 16 or turn right for the tastiest pasta 17. Turn left on Via dei Tre Pupazzi for a drink with a view 18. Continue and turn left again on Via Alberico II. Turn right and take the first left on Via Crescenzio for a drink at a mysterious bar 19. Turn right and once again cross Piazza del Risorgimento for the tastiest tiramisu 20. Turn left on Via Catone and turn right at Via Germanico for some shopping 21. Turn left on Via Silla and continue to Via Cola de Rienzo. Turn left here for a culinary souvenir 22. Take a quick detour onto Via Fabio Massimo for a gelato 23 and then head back to the mall for more shopping 24 25. Turn left on Via Atilio Regolo for a cute bakery 26 or walk down the street for a cool Japanese restaurant 27. Return to Cola di Rienzo by way of Via Ezio for more great stores 28 29 30. Turn right at the traffic light to follow Piazza della Liberta and bear right on Via Federico Cesi. On the first street on the right you will find a cool streetwear boutique 31. Walk down Via Federico Cesi until you are surrounded by palm trees 32. Walk past the Corte Suprema di Cassazione 33 to Via Vittoria Colonna for the tastiest Neapolitan pizza 34. Walk right along the Tiber, turn right, and take a detour for a photo on the bridge 35 before sitting down on the cozy terrace of Bibliobar 36. Then visit Castel Sant'Angelo 37. Finish on Ponte Sant'Angelo 38, which connects Castel Sant'Angelo with Centro Storico.

SIGHTS & ATTRACTIONS

3 It all started with the private collection of Pope Julius II, the Renaissance Pope, who wanted to reinstate Rome as the center of the art world. Each pope thereafter expanded the collection, and new galleries were built to house all the artwork. To this day the **Musei Vaticani** (Vatican Museums) comprise the largest, richest, and most impressive museum complex in the world. There are more than fourteen hundred rooms filled with paintings, Greek and Roman sculptures, and Egyptian and Etruscan art.

Viale Vaticano, museivaticani.va, open Mon-Sat 9am-6pm (admittance until 4pm), May-Oct Fri 9am-10:30pm (admittance until 8:30pm) & Sat 9am-8pm (admittance until 6pm), last Sun of the month 9am-2pm (admittance until 12:30pm), €17 + reservation costs (obligatory), last Sun of the month free, Metro to Ottaviano, Tram 19 Risorgimento/S. Pietro

4 The gigantic pinecone **Cortile della Pigna** dates to the 1st century BCE and was found on the Campo Marzio, near the Pantheon. It came from the Baths of Agrippa and was originally a fountain. The peacocks are copies of antique statues that were located at Hadrian's mausoleum. Bramante designed this courtyard.

Part of Musei Vaticani, Metro to Ottaviano, Tram 19 Risorgimento/S. Pietro

5 The ceiling of the **Galleria degli Arazzi** (Gallery of Tapestries) is painted, but the wall decorations are woven. The unique tapestry on the left as you enter the room was designed by Raphael for the Sistine Chapel. Pay attention to *The Resurrection of Christ*: wherever you stand in the gallery, the eyes of Jesus appear to follow you.

Part of Musei Vaticani, Metro to Ottaviano, Tram 19 Risorgimento/S. Pietro

6 The **Galleria delle Carte Geografiche** (Gallery of Maps) has the largest collection of geographical paintings in the world. The maps were made in the 16th century by the monk Ignazio Danti. Just reflect for a second about when they were made, and then realize how absurdly accurate they actually are. We still don't understand how Danti did it.

Part of Musei Vaticani, Metro to Ottaviano, Tram 19 Risorgimento/S. Pietro

14
S·APOST PAVLVS·V·BVRGHESIVS·ROMANVS·PONT·MAX·AN·MDCX

38

6

7 Pope Julius II did not like the idea of living in the quarters of his predecessor, so he had new rooms decorated. The young but very talented painter Raphael from Urbino, who was just twenty-five years old, was given the honor of decorating the rooms with intricate frescos. The contiguous rooms have gone down in history as **Raphael Rooms** (Stanze di Raffaello), the most famous being the *Room of the Signatura* with the School of Athens philosophers.
Part of Musei Vaticani, Metro to Ottaviano, Tram 19 Risorgimento/S. Pietro

8 The **Sistine Chapel** (Cappella Sistina) is the pope's private chapel. Michelangelo painted the ceiling al fresco with what would become one of the most famous images in art history: *The Creation of Adam* depicts God, with Eve and the first generation of people, floating in a backdrop strikingly similar to the shape of a human brain. Michelangelo created the ceiling fresco in two installments, beginning at the back of the chapel. He had sheets hung everywhere because he did not want to be watched, and the story goes that he even chased away the pope with his brushes. When Michelangelo saw the finished scenes, he decided the other images need to be a bit larger. Later he returned to paint *The Last Judgment* on the wall behind the altar.
Part of Musei Vaticani, Metro to Ottaviano, Tram 19 Risorgimento/S. Pietro

9 The stairs you take to leave Musei Vaticani were commissioned by Pope Pius XI and designed by architect Giuseppe Momo, in the first half of the 20th century. **Scala Elicoidale Momo** (Momo's spiral staircase) is one of the most photographed stairs in the world, and with reason. They consist of a double ramp, allowing visitors to walk in both directions without crossing each other. Momo's stairs look like another set of stairs in the museum: Scala del Bramante. It is said the pope was so inspired by Bramante's stairs, that he had Giuseppe Momo's design altered.
Part of Musei Vaticani, Metro to Ottaviano, Tram 19 Risorgimento/S. Pietro

13 The colonnades on **Piazza San Pietro** are Bernini's masterpiece. He worked on them from 1655 until 1667, and to this day people are speechless when they see them. There are 284 columns divided into four rows. Look for the round stones between the obelisk and the fountains—when standing here, the four rows seem to melt into one. The obelisk in the middle of the square is the

oldest monument here. It was transported to Rome in 36 CE. In 2019 the 20-foot-high (6 m) Angels Unawares monument was erected on the square in memory of all immigrants and refugees. The pope holds his weekly audience every Wednesday morning on the square. Free tickets can be obtained at the bronze gate in the colonnade on the right until one day in advance.
Piazza San Pietro, Metro to Ottaviano, Tram 19 Risorgimento/S. Pietro

14 **St. Peter's Basilica** (Basilica di San Pietro) was built atop St. Peter's tomb, where a previous church had been constructed around 400 CE. Today it is the largest church in the world. It was Pope Julius II who, in 1506, ordered the construction of the current basilica. He called in the help of artists such as Bramante, Raphael, Michelangelo—who designed the beautiful dome—and Bernini. *The Pietà* in the first chapel on the right is magnificent. Michelangelo sculpted it when he was just twenty-four.
Piazza San Pietro, vatican.va, open Apr-Sep 7am-7pm, Oct-Mar 7am-6:30pm, free, Metro to Ottaviano, Tram 19 Risorgimento/S. Pietro

33 The Romans are not huge fans of this big box of a building. In their opinion, **Corte Suprema di Cassazione** (Palace of Justice) is too much of everything: it's too big, too full, the ornaments are too large, and it's overwhelming and obtrusive. These are enough reasons for Romans to give the building the nickname "palazzaccio," which means the ugly palace. Seen from across the Tiber on Via Giuseppe Zanardelli, the palace looks like it's just on the other side of the street, without the river flowing in between.
Piazza Cavour, not open to the public, Metro to Lepanto, Bus to Piazza Cavour

37 **Castel Sant'Angelo** (Castle of the Holy Angel) was commissioned by the Roman emperor Hadrian as a mausoleum for himself and his family. Its strategic position made it a part of the Aurelian wall, and later it was used as a prison and a fortress. Around 1500, Pope Alexander VI started restorations on the castle, and it became a summer palace for the papacy. The name of the castle dates from the late 6th century when, according to legend, the Archangel Michael appeared to Pope Gregorius I as a sign that the plague had ended.
Lungotevere Castello 50, castelsantangelo.com, open Tue-Sun 9am-7:30pm, €14, Metro to Lepanto, Tram 19 Risorgimento/S. Pietro

38 The **Ponte Sant'Angelo** is one of the most beautiful bridges over the Tiber River. Look up to see Bernini's angels, which carry symbols of the Passion of Christ, such as the pillar on which he was flogged and the nails that fastened him to the cross. Two of these angels were deemed too beautiful to be outside. They were moved to Sant'Andrea delle Fratte, and copies were placed on the bridge to weather the elements.

Ponte Sant'Angelo, Metro to Ottaviano, Tram 19 Risorgimento/S. Pietro

FOOD & DRINK

1 There's no better way to start the day in Rome than with a good cup of coffee and a crispy cornetto. **Trecaffè** is passionate and well-practiced in the art of making coffee, so there's no better place to start than here. For a heartier breakfast, try the eggs on avocado toast.

Via Leone IV 10, tel. 06-39723466, trecaffe.it, open Mon-Sat 6:30am-4:30pm, Sun 7am-4pm, coffee €1.50, cornetto €2, Metro to Ottaviano

2 You may need some extra energy before you start your tour of the Musei Vaticani! **Re-Bio** is the ideal place to load up on local and organic juices, sandwiches, and salads. They also have several vegan options.
Via Germanico 59, tel. 06-39746510, rebio.it, open Mon-Wed 7:30am-6pm, Thu-Sat 7:30am-11pm, last Sun of the month 7:30am-6pm, €9, Metro to Ottaviano

11 After a visit to the Vatican, you won't have to walk far for lunch. At **200°** they are serious about their bread and bake it in a 200° Celsius oven. Choose from a variety of sandwiches with clever names such as "Pietà" and "Colosseo."
Piazza del Risorgimento 3, tel. 06-39754239, duecentogradi.it, open Mon-Thu 10-3am, Fri-Sat 10-4am, Sun 11-3am, sandwich €7.50, Metro to Ottaviano, Tram 19 Risorgimento/S. Pietro

12 Located in the upscale Prati neighborhood, **La Zanzara** ("mosquito") is a beautiful bistro with a Paris-meets-Rome vibe. Hipsters and office workers flock

here throughout the day, making it a busy and vibrant place to hang out. The aperitivo is an especially fun way to start your evening.

Via Crescenzio 84, tel. 06-68392227, lazanzararoma.com, open Tue-Sat noon-1am, Sun noon-6pm, €24, Metro to Ottaviano, Tram 19 Risorgimento/S. Pietro

16 A traditional osteria is a place to drink wine and have a simple meal. **Borgosteria** is not just any osteria—it's a modern-day version with a retro interior and an open kitchen. Come here for a delicious pasta or risotto, good wine, and desserts that are so yummy, it's a good thing you've been walking all day.

Borgo Pio 161, tel. 06-64760245, open Mon-Sat noon-10:30pm, €16, Metro to Ottaviano, Tram 19 Risorgimento/S. Pietro

17 **Borghiciana Pastificio Artigianale** is a cute little pasta place with an inviting but somewhat chaotically planted green façade, where there's always a line out the door. The food, served on fantastic and colorful dishes, is very well prepared, and the place itself has a cozy vibe.

Borgo Pio 186, borghicianapastificioartigianale.business.site, open Mon-Wed & Fri-Sat 9am-6pm, Thu 9am-10pm, €11, Tram 19 Risorgimento/S. Pietro

18 If you go to Les Étoiles, you must visit the eighth floor's special rooftop patio. **Terrazza Les Étoiles** is old-fashioned chic, a bit over the top, but with an unmistakable charm. From here you have the best view of the dome of the Basilica di San Pietro. The bill will be pricey, but just take another look at the dome to remind yourself that it's worth it.

Via dei Bastioni 1, tel. 06-686386, terrazzalesetoiles.com, open daily 10am-midnight, glass wine €12, cocktail €18, Metro to Ottaviano, Tram 19 Risorgimento/S. Pietro

19 This is a unique bar; it's like visiting an art-collecting explorer from days gone by. **Emerald's Independent Bar** is open from aperitivo time until the last cocktail, often with live music. They also serve small bites.

Via Crescenzio 91c, tel. 06-88654275, emeraldsbar.it, open daily 6:30pm-2am, cocktail €15, Metro to Ottaviano, Tram 19 Risorgimento/S. Pietro

20 Tiramisu is on almost every menu you see, and it's one of Italy's most famous desserts. There are multiple stories about its origin, and there has always been a friendly rivalry between the regions Friuli and Veneto about where the first tiramisu came from. What everyone does agree on is that it's a fantastic dessert. **Pompi** sells not only the classic version of tiramisu, but also surprising flavors like banana-chocolate or salted caramel.
Piazza del Risorgimento 43, tel. 06-39737088, barpompi.it, open Mon-Thu 8am-11pm, Fri-Sat 8am-midnight, Sun 9am-11pm, tiramisu €5, Metro to Ottaviano, Tram 19 Risorgimento/S. Pietro

23 On a side street in the heart of Prati is **Guttilla Alta Gelateria Italiana.** This is the place for a refreshing gelato in a cone, a cup, on a stick, or as an ice praline. Then, you can choose which filling you like in your cone: pure, white, or pistachio chocolate.
Via dei Gracchi 93, tel. 06-66006209, guttilla.it, open Mon-Thu & Sun 11am-mignight, Fri-Sat 11-1am, gelato €3, Metro to Ottaviano, Tram 19 Risorgimento/S. Pietro

26 For more than forty years, artisan bakery **Il Gianfornaio** has been serving Roman families with freshly baked bread, cakes, and pancakes on Sunday. Nowadays you can also have lunch or order a fresh smoothie. Try the crispy pizza al taglio (pizza cut to size).
Via dei Gracchi 179, tel. 06-3231811, ilgianfornaio.com, open Mon-Sat 7:30am-9pm, Sun 9am-9pm, coffee €2.10, Metro to Lepanto, Tram 19 Lepanto

27 International cuisine is not very well represented in Rome, but **Chopstick** is an exception. With its colorful and extravagant interior, it's a traditional Japanese restaurant with a very untraditional flourish.
Via dei Gracchi 264, tel. 346-323-0063, chopstickprati.com, open Mon-Fri 12:30-15pm & 7pm-midnight, Sat-Sun 12:30-4pm & 7:30pm-midnight, lunch €24, Metro to Lepanto, Tram 19 Lepanto

34 Salvatore di Matteo Le Gourmet, **Salvatore** for short, has the best Neapolitan pizzas. They are made with a fluffy dough, and all the toppings are

36

12

delicious, although Italians will always tell you pizza Margherita is the best choice.

Via Vittoria Colonna 32a, tel. 06-86766621, open Mon-Sat 7:30am-11pm, Sun 8-11:30am, pizza €9, Metro to Lepanto, Tram 19 Risorgimento/S. Pietro

36 The terrace of **Bibliobar** is a special place to sit down and relax. It offers a view of the imposing Ponte Sant'Angelo on one side and the gigantic Corte Suprema di Cassazione on the other. Enjoy this scenic place while sipping a coffee or a glass of wine.

Lungotevere Castello, tel. 340-941-9288, open Mon-Thu & Sun 7:30am-10pm, Fri-Sat 7:30-2am, coffee €1, Metro to Lepanto

SHOPPING

21 **Port à Demìe** (or PAD) is a great boutique for women's clothing, with well-known and beautiful clothing brands. The store is roomy and light, the service is friendly, and the collections are modern and innovative.

Via Silla 32, portademie.com, open Mon 3:30-7:30pm, Tue-Sat 10:30am-7:30pm, Metro to Ottaviano, Tram 19 Ottaviano

22 It was in 1913 when Giacinto Callipo established his company in the tuna business in Calabria, in Southern Italy. **Callipo** is still a big name in specialized canned seafood. Here on Via Cola di Rienzo you can buy cans or glass jars of tuna in all different shapes and sizes. They are sold in fun packaging and look great in the kitchen.

Via Cola di Rienzo 248, callipo.com, open daily 10am-8pm, Metro to Ottaviano, Tram 19 Risorgimento/S. Pietro

24 **Castroni** has been around since the 1930s, and over the years the offerings have expanded significantly. The shop introduced soy sauce and coconut milk to Rome in the 1950s. Today, people go to Castroni for the vintage feel: you can experience groceries as they were in the times of *La Dolce Vita*.

Via Cola di Rienzo 196-198, castronicoladirienzo.com, open daily 8:30am-8pm, Metro to Ottaviano, Tram 19 Risorgimento/S. Pietro

25 **Coin Excelsior** is a beautiful department store on the most popular shopping street for locals, **Cola di Rienzo,** where many fantastic (Italian) brands are sold. At Coin Excelsior (and not its little sister, Coin) you find the most beautiful makeup and skin-care products, home accessories, clothing, and gadgets.
Via Cola di Rienzo 173, coin.it, open daily 10am-8pm, Metro to Lepanto, Tram 19 Risorgimento/S. Pietro

28 Welcome to ballerina heaven or **BallereTTe.** These flat shoes were designed in Rome and sold only in shops in Italy—chances are you won't see anyone with the same shoes back home.
Piazza Cola di Rienzo 91, www.ballerette.com/en_us, open daily 10am-8pm, Metro to Levanto, Tram 19 Levanto

29 The best Italian espresso at home is made in a moka, and the best place to buy one is at **Bialetti Home.** Depending on how much coffee you want to make, there are different sizes. So you might see a few mokas alongside each other in the average Italian household. If you have extra space in your suitcase, you'll want to take one or two home with you.
Piazza Cola di Rienzo 82, bialetti.com, open daily 9:15am-8pm, Metro to Lepanto, Tram 19 Lepanto

30 If you want to wear what young Roman women are wearing, visit **Iron G Superstore.** Clothing in this shop is feminine, trendy, colorful, and very affordable. Is clothing not what you're looking for? Then look at the fun handbags, shoes, and jewelry.
Via Cola di Rienzo 50, open Mon-Sat 10am-7:30pm, Sun 11am-2:30 pm & 3:30-7:30pm, Metro to Lepanto

31 Fun, funky, and edgy—all words that describe **Kozmo Laze.** They specialize in sneakers, and they are very careful about choosing which sneakers to sell. The result is fantastic and unique sneakers for men and women that also delights the staff. This shop is their playground; sneakers are painted, there's an arcade in the shop, and they throw parties.
Via Federico Cesi 54, www.kozmolaze.com/en, open daily 10am-8pm, Metro to Lepanto, Tram 19 Lepanto

benedica questa casa
Papa Francesco
Pensiamo che bello è essere santi, ma che bello è essere perdonati
Papa Francesco
PAPA FRANCESCO
San Giovanni Paolo II
Papa Francesco
Francesco
PAPA FRANCESCO
13 MARZO 2013
Benedici la nostra casa
Una catena di impegno per la pace unisca tutti gli uomini e le donne di buona volontà!
Francesco
Alzi forte in tutta la terra il grido della pace!
PAPA FRANCESCO
PAPA FRANCESCO
Papa Francesco
Se Dio non perdonasse tutto, il mondo non esisterebbe
Papa Francesco
JOHN PAUL II - FRANCIS - JOHN XXIII
PAPA FRANCESCO
Papa Francesco
Benedici la nostra casa
Papa Francesco
Che Dio benedica questa casa
PAPA FRANCESCO
MADE IN ITALY
La carità, la pazienza

32

MORE TO EXPLORE

10 If you want to visit the **Giardini Vaticani** (Vatican Gardens), you must make reservations online two days in advance. The extensive gardens occupy about half the area of Vatican City, and the tour takes approximately two hours. On the tour, you'll see the romantic English garden decorated with remnants of pillars and sculptures from the villas of Nero and Caligula, as well as the pope's helipad, the transmitter tower of Radio Vaticana, and a replica of the caves at Lourdes, France.

Viale Vaticano, museivaticani.va, tours Mon-Tue & Thu-Sat, €32, Metro to Ottaviano, Tram 19 Risorgimento/S. Pietro

15 Once you buy your ticket for the **Cupola of St. Peter's Basilica** (Cupola della Basilica di San Pietro), you can walk up all the way or take an elevator to the first observation deck at 175 feet (53 m). Here, from the gallery at the base of the dome, you will absorb, once again, how big it is. Next, you can get to the top via stairs inside the dome. Take your time if you decide to go up on foot—there are 551 steps, and the view is more than worth it.

Piazza San Pietro, vatican.va, open Apr-Sep 8am-6pm, Oct-Mar 8am-5pm, stairs €8, lift + stairs €10, Metro to Ottaviano, Tram 19 Risorgimento/S. Pietro

32 The beautiful **Piazza Cavour** is named after Italy's first prime minister, Camillo Benso, Count of Cavour. His statue was unveiled in 1895 by King Umberto I in honor of the twentieth anniversary of the liberation of Rome. Thanks to the palm trees, the sleekly designed square looks a lot more relaxed, making it a wonderful place to sit for a while.

Piazza Cavour, Metro to Lepanto, Bus to Piazza Cavour

35 Stop for a short while on **Ponte Umberto I** before you proceed to an outdoor restaurant to start your evening. Walk to the end of the bridge, turn toward Castel Sant'Angelo, and enjoy the breathtaking view. The bridge connects the Prati and the Ponte districts.

Ponte Umberto I, Bus to Zanardelli

WALK 5

REPUBBLICA, TRIDENTE & VILLA BORGHESE

ABOUT THE WALK

This walk includes impressive monuments and theatrical backdrops against which Roman life plays out. The walk begins at Piazza della Repubblica, where you can still see just how big Diocleitian's baths once were. Enjoy the view as you descend Quirinale (Quirinal Hill) and enjoy your passeggiata (walk) through the Rome you've seen in the movies.

THE NEIGHBORHOODS

You'll start your walk at Palazzo Massimo and continue through the grand **Piazza della Repubblica** to the Santa Maria della Concezione dei Cappuccini, which is decorated with the bones and skulls of 3,600 Capuchin friars—yes, it's a bit macabre.

With the **Fontana dell'Acqua Felice,** a trend was started that every pope wanted to follow: installing an insanely impressive monument (fountains were especially popular) to leave the city more beautiful than they had found it. Among the popes was Barberini Pope Urban VIII. His building frenzy can be witnessed in **Piazza Barberini** as well as at the **Galleria Nazionale di Palazzo Barberini.**

Over Quirinal Hill and past the world-famous **Trevi Fountain,** you will find the chic shopping street **Via dei Condotti** that leads to **Piazza di Spagna,** where father and son Bernini worked together on the famous and peculiar boat fountain, La Barcaccia, at the foot of the Spanish Steps.

Then you'll wind down two historic streets: **Via Vittoria** connects Via del Corso and Via del Babuino and is known as the most perfumed street in Rome; and **Via Margutta** has an eclectic feel and is located between the Piazza di Spagna and the impressive **Piazza del Popolo.** In Piazza del Popolo look for the

Tridente: the three streets that diverge from each other to form Neptune's trident. Admire the Egyptian obelisk (brought to Rome by the ancient Romans) and the works of Raphael, Caravaggio, and Bernini in the Santa Maria del Popolo, and then climb up **Monte Pincio.**

Villa Borghese is a green respite. This was once the backyard of Cardinal Scipione Borghese, whose art collection is housed in the **Galleria Borghese.** It includes Bernini's four dynamic statues, which are must-sees.

SHORT ON TIME? HERE ARE THE HIGHLIGHTS:
10 SANTA MARIA DELLA CONCEZIONE DEI CAPPUCCINI + 16 TREVI FOUNTAIN + 20 PIAZZA DI SPAGNA + 26 VIA MARGUTTA + 34 VILLA BORGHESE

REPUBBLICA, TRIDENTE & VILLA BORGHESE

1 Palazzo Massimo
2 Caffetteria Massimo
3 HummusTown Kiosk
4 Piazza della Repubblica
5 Santa Maria degli Angeli e dei Martiri
6 Fontana dell'Acqua Felice
7 Santa Maria della Vittoria
8 Come il Latte
9 Elsa Coffee
10 **Santa Maria della Concezione dei Cappuccini**
11 Fontana del Tritone
12 Galleria Nazionale di Palazzo Barberini
13 San Carlo alle Quattro Fontane
14 Palazzo del Quirinale
15 Baccano
16 **Trevi Fountain**
17 Rinascente
18 DEROMA
19 Ginger
20 **Piazza di Spagna**
21 Babingtons Tea Room
22 Via Vittoria
23 La Buvette
24 Ara Pacis
25 Canova Tadolini
26 **Via Margutta**
27 Il Marmoraro
28 Babette
29 Holypopstore
30 Buccone Vini e Olii
31 Piazza del Popolo
32 Santa Maria del Popolo
33 Giardino del Pincio
34 **Villa Borghese**
35 Tempio di Esculapio
36 Galleria Borghese
37 Marziali 1922

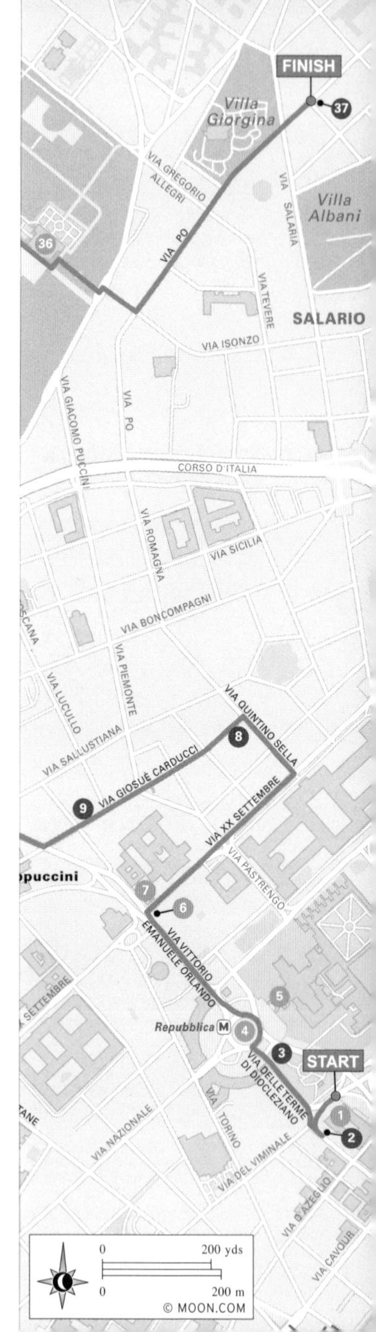

WALK 5 DESCRIPTION (approx. 7mi/11 km)

Start at Palazzo Massimo 1 and have a coffee 2. Then walk along the park for a Middle Eastern snack 3 to Piazza della Repubblica 4 with Michelangelo's last work 5. Turn right as you exit the church and walk to the intersection for a fountain and a church 6 7. Turn right on Via Venti Settembre, turn left on Via Quintino Sella, and take a left on Via Giosuè Carducci for gelato 8 or coffee 9. Turn right at Via Leonida Bissolati, turn left at the second major intersection, and walk along Via Vittorio Veneto to visit a unique church 10. Continue left as you exit the chapel and walk across the square 11. Go left on Via Delle Quattro Fontane to find the palace of Barberini 12. At the intersection with the four fountains is a small but imposing church 13. Walk to the square with the obelisk 14. Turn right on Via della Dataria, bear left on Via dell'Umiltà, and turn right and immediately left for a pleasant bistro 15. Walk up Via delle Muratte to the Trevi Fountain 16. Then turn left on Via della Panetteria and right on Via del Tritone to shop at a department store and an excavation 17. Walk back a bit to Via del Nazareno, turn left at Largo del Nazareno, and left on Via Poli for coffee 18. Walk back and continue on Via del Pozzetto. Turn right, cross Piazza di San Silvestro, and continue on Via del Gambero. Turn left on Via Borgognona for a healthy lunch 19. Turn left at the end of the street and immediately turn right again for the chic shopping street Via dei Condotti. Continue to the square in front of the Spanish Steps 20 where you can have a cup of tea 21. Turn left for the most perfumed street 22 and a delicious pasta 23. Walk all the way down to the Tiber and visit the altar of peace in a modern structure 24. Turn left on Via Tomacelli and turn left again to shop along Via del Corso. Turn right on Via di S. Giacomo and right again for coffee in a former art studio 25 or walk straight ahead and buy a tablet with a Roman saying in the city's bohemian alley 26 27. Walk down farther for a French-Italian fusion restaurant 28. Turn left on Via del Corso, take the first right, and walk on for sneakers 29. Walk back slightly and turn left for a glass of wine 30 or continue to the square with the obelisk 31. The church has a unique history 32. Climb the hill and enjoy the panorama 33. Walk through the huge park to the romantic lake 34 35 and some magnificent art 36. Exit the park, turn left, and complete the walk with something sweet 37.

SIGHTS & ATTRACTIONS

1 The art at **Palazzo Massimo** includes Roman statues, sarcophagi, frescoes, and mosaics that were unearthed in 1870, as modern Rome was constructed to serve as Italy's capital. Arranged chronologically and according to theme, the collection is like walking through an art history book.
Largo Villa Peretti 2, museonazionaleromano.beniculturali.it/palazzo-massimo, open Tue-Sun 9:30am-7pm, Combi ticket Museo Nazionale Romano €11, Metro A, B, B1 Termini, Tram 5, 14 Termini

4 **Piazza della Repubblica** used to be called Piazza Esedra, after the large, semi-circular niche that was part of the Baths of Diocletian. More than 150 years ago, during the unification of Italy, architect Gaetano Koch was commissioned to revamp this square. He paid homage to the ancient shapes with two neoclassical colonnades. The Fontana delle Naiadi (Fountain of Water Nymphs) was designed by Alessandro Guerrieri in 1885.
Piazza della Repubblica, Metro to Republicca, Tram 5, 14 Termini

5 Emperor Diocleitian's gigantic bathhouse complex was the largest in antiquity. After the fall of the Roman Empire and the later invasion of the Goths, the complex fell out of use. The area around the baths was hardly inhabited, and water could no longer be supplied. Halfway through the 16th century a priest saw light radiate up from the ruins, and in the light were seven martyrs. The priest saw this as a sign that a church should be dedicated here to those martyrs. Three popes later, Pope Pius IV finally agreed with him. Michelangelo had the honor of designing the **Santa Maria degli Angeli e dei Martiri.** He was eighty-six at the time and never saw the finished church.
Piazza Della Repubblica, santamariadegliangeliroma.it, open daily 10am-1pm & 4-7pm, free, Metro to Republicca, Tram 5, 14 Termini

6 Pope Sixtus V (from 1585) supported urban planning by having new streets built and aqueducts refurbished. The **Fontana dell'Acqua Felice** was built to celebrate the opening of one of the aqueducts. Sculptor Leonardo Sormani used ancient Roman columns and added Egyptian lions, and the pope also

16
CLEMENS XII·PONT·MAX·
AQVAM VIRGINEM
COPIA ET SALVBRITATE COMMENDATAM
CVLTV MAGNIFICO ORNAVIT
ANNO DOMINI MDCCXXXV·PONTIF·VI·

added a statue of Moses. It was this addition that gave the fountain its painful nickname: Mosè ridicolo, or Moses the ridiculous.

Piazza Della Repubblica, Metro to Republicca, Tram 5, 14 Termini

7 As you step inside the **Santa Maria della Vittoria,** the baroque décor might be overwhelming. Bernini's beautiful sculpture, *Ecstasy of Saint Theresa,* can be found in the last chapel on the left before the main altar. Here, an angel pierces her with a spear and makes her body glow with pleasure. Opposite is Saint Vittoria, the Roman martyr and namesake of the church, who lays in a glass coffin so the miracle of her imperishable body is well in view.

Via Venti Settembre 17, turismoroma.it/en/places/church-santa-maria-della-vittoria, open Mon-Sat 9am-noon & 2:30-6pm, Sun 15:30-6pm, free, Metro to Republicca, Tram 5, 14 Termini

10 **Santa Maria delle Concezione dei Cappuccini** (crypt of the Capuchins) hides a macabre scene: the bones of about four thousand monks are displayed inside the chapel. The reason for this is unclear: some suggest they were meant

to be decorative; others posit that the bones were moved to make room in the tombs.

Via Vittorio Veneto 27, cappucciniviaveneto.it, open daily 10am-7pm, €11.50, Metro to Barberini, Tram 5, 14 Termini

11 In the middle of Piazza Barberini is the Bernini-designed **Fontana del Tritone** (Triton Fountain). Commissioned by Pope Urban VIII, it features four dolphins holding up a seashell, upon which a muscular Triton kneels with a conch shell to his lips. From this, a jet of water spews up high into the air. The fountain base features a depiction of bees—a symbol of the powerful Barberini family.

Piazza Barberini, Metro to Barberini

12 The Barberini family bought a small house from the Farnese family in 1625, who had bought it from the Della Rovere family. The Barberinis remodeled it extensively—most notable are the stairwells by Borromini and Bernini. The **Galleria Nazionale di Palazzo Barberini** houses works by Cosimo, Bronzino, Lorenzo Lotto, Tintoretto, Caravaggio (don't miss his beautiful *Narciccus*), Reni, Poussin, and Van Wittel (pronounced "Vanvitelli" in Italian). Among the loveliest pieces in the collection is Raphael's *Fornarina*.

Via delle Quattro Fontane 13, barberinicorsini.org, open Tue-Sun 10am-7pm, €13, Metro to Barberini

13 Though Roman architecture tends toward grandeur, **San Carlo alle Quattro Fontane** shows that bigger is not always better. Also called San Carlino because of its size, this little church was built by Borromini, who used all his skills to make the small building as imposing as possible. It is one of the best examples of Baroque architecture in the world.

Via del Quirinale 23, sancarlino.eu, open Mon-Sat 10am-1pm, free, Metro to Barberini

14 The Piazza del Quirinale offers a fantastic view of Rome and the dome of the Basilica di San Pietro. At 200 feet (61 m), Quirinal Hill is the highest of Rome's seven hills. The fountain on the square incorporates old Roman statues of Castor and Pollux and an Egyptian obelisk added in the 18th century. The enormous **Palazzo del Quirinale** was built in the 16th century as a summer house for the pope. It served as the royal palace for a long time, and since 1947

it has been the official residence of the president of the Italian Republic. You can book a visit through the website.
Piazza del Quirinale, palazzo.quirinale.it, open Tue-Wed & Fri-Sun 9:30am-4:30pm (last admittance 2:30pm), €1.50 per tour, Metro to Barberini, Tram 8 Venezia

16 Anita Ekberg's midnight swim in the **Trevi Fountain** (Fontana di Trevi) is world famous, but don't try to imitate this scene from the movie *La Dolce Vita*—bathing in the ornately decorated rococo fountain is prohibited. The water flows through an aqueduct dating to ancient Roman times. The origin of the fountain's name is unresolved: it could derive from the virgin Trivia who, according to legend, pointed out the water source in ancient Rome or from Trivium, the three streets that converge onto the square where the fountain is located. Toss a coin into the fountain with your right hand over your left shoulder or vice versa, and the story goes that when you do this, you will one day return to Rome.
Piazza Fontana di Trevi, Metro to Barberini, Tram 8 Venezia

20 Take a seat on the Spanish Steps and watch the countless tourists taking pictures. There are 138 steps that connect the Trinità dei Monti church to the rest of the city, and at the top they offer a view of **Piazza di Spagna,** named after the 17th century Palazzo di Spagna, which was home to the Spanish embassy.
Piazza di Spagna, Metro to Spagna, Tram 2 Flaminio

24 **Ara Pacis** (peace altar) was built between 19 and 9 BCE in honor of the stability brought back to the Roman world by Emperor Augustus. The marble reliefs depict Augustus and the imperial family, as well as senators, priests, and gods. After the Roman Empire fell, the altar was looted. Many years later, after years of international negotiations, the pieces were returned and the altar restored.
Lungotevere in Augusta/corner of Via Tomacelli, open daily 9:30am-7:30pm, €15, Metro to Spagna, Tram 2 Flaminio

31 At one time, the Porta del Popolo, at the northern end of **Piazza del Popolo,** was the most important entry gate to the city, as many visitors came from the north. Bernini refurbished the gate significantly in honor of the arrival of Swedish queen Christina, who abdicated the throne and spent the rest of her

13

36

life in Rome. The Egyptian obelisk in the center of the piazza was moved from the Circo Massimo.

Piazza del Popolo, Metro to Flaminio, Tram 2 Flaminio

32 Supposedly the church **Santa Maria del Popolo** was built at the location where Emperor Nero died. The story goes that a walnut tree grew in the spot, and it was occupied by evil spirits. In the 11th century, the pope ended it all by chopping down the tree and building a chapel in its place. Bramante designed the shell-shaped altar, and Raphael designed a family chapel for Agostino Chigi (the second chapel in the left). In the same chapel you can admire Bernini's *Habakuk and the Angel.* In the back left of the church, two masterpieces by Caravaggio depict the patron saints of Rome: Peter and Paul.

Piazza del Popolo, open Mon-Thu 7:15am-12:30pm & 4-7pm, Fri-Sat 7:30am-7pm, Sun 7:30am-1:30pm & 4:30-7:30pm, free, Metro to Flaminio, Tram 2 Flaminio

36 **Galleria Borghese** showcases artwork from Cardinal Scipione Borghese's private collection. Cardinal Borghese gave Bernini his first major commission of four monumental statues, and he also obtained the works of other famous artists, including Caravaggio—these came into his possession for a small price after Caravaggio's teacher in Rome, Giuseppe Cesari, was imprisoned by Borghese's uncle the pope.
Piazzale del Museo Borghese, gebart.it/musei/galleria-borghese, open Tue-Sun 9am-7pm (reservations required), €15, Bus to Pinciano/Museo Borghese

FOOD & DRINK

2 **Caffetteria Massimo** opened in the Palazzo Massimo in 2021. It's a modern and minimalistic lunchroom where you can have a coffee and a sandwich either before or after your visit to the museum.
Via Giovanni Amendola 6, tel. 06-4885617, open Tue-Sun 11am-6pm, €10, Metro A, B, B1 Termini, Tram 5, 14 Termini

3 The nonprofit organization HummusTown's motto is, "It tastes like home," which refers to the Middle Eastern cuisine they sell at **HummusTown Kiosk.** The organization was founded in 2018 with the purpose of helping Syrian refugees find gainful employment as well as introduce the Roman population to Syrian food. Try the hummus, falafel, shawarma, and the delicious coffee.
Viale Luigi Einaudi, tel. 389-893-0310, hummustown.com, open daily 8am-11pm, €7, Metro to Republicca, Tram 5, 14 Termini

8 This fancy gelateria, **Come il Latte,** serves extra creamy gelato that consists of 60 to 70 percent milk. It is made fresh daily with organic eggs and seasonal produce sourced locally. Try the artisanal cono artigianale—an extra crunchy cone.
Via Silvio Spaventa 24-26, tel. 06-42903882, comeillatte.it, open Mon-Thu & Sun noon-11pm, Fri-Sat noon-midnight, gelato €3, Metro to Barberini, Tram 5, 14 Termini

9 **Elsa Coffee** is a traditional coffee bar between Termini station and Villa Borghese, near the famous Via Veneto. It's a great place for either a relaxed Italian-style coffee break or for a quick espresso at the bar.
Via Giosuè Carducci 30, tel. 06-42011887, open Mon-Sat 6am-7pm, Sun 7am-1pm, cappuccino €1, Metro to Barberini, Tram 5, 14 Termini

15 **Baccano** feels like a Parisian bistro with a New York flair. The menu features both classic Italian and international favorites. Come here for lunch, aperitivo, and dinner.
Via delle Muratte 23, tel. 06-69941166, baccanoroma.com, open daily noon-midnight, €28, Metro to Barberini, Tram 8 Venezia

18 While you twirl your fork in an authentic Roman pasta at **DEROMA,** you can partake in some pretty good people-watching from this corner establishment's sidewalk patio. Inside, the décor evokes the glamour of the Dolce Vita years. In addition to pastas, there are oysters with exciting dressings, meats from the grill, and large salads. If you want just a quick bite, you can visit the bakery.
Via Poli 27, tel. 06-89685899, deromamor.com, open daily 8-1am, €24, Metro to Barberini, Tram 8 Venezia

19 With two locations in central Rome, **Ginger** is the place to go for a tasty salad, smoothie, or sandwich. The location near Piazza di Spagna is spacious, with lots of indoor and outdoor tables. You can also order your food to go.
Via Borgognona 43-46, tel. 06-69940836, gingersaporiesalute.com, open daily 9:30am-11:30pm, salad €15, Metro to Spagna, Tram 2 Flaminio

21 Right now the fourth generation is at the helm of **Babingtons Tea Room,** as it's been around for more than a hundred years. Elizabeth Taylor, Audrey Hepburn, and Federico Fellini all came here to drink their tea. Back in the day, Rome was an obligatory stop for young and wealthy British during their grand tours, and a cup of tea after sightseeing was called for.
Piazza di Spagna 23, tel. 06-6786027, babingtons.com, open Mon & Wed-Sun 10am-11pm, high tea €32, Metro to Spagna, Tram 2 Flaminio

VINI
BACCANO

25

23 **La Buvette** is a great place to take a breather. It has a vintage feel with wood wainscoting, leather sofas, and a menu packed full of Roman, Italian, and international classics, such as pastas and wok stir-fries. The outside tables, if you can snag one, make a great spot for people-watching.
Via Vittoria 44/47, tel. 06-6790383, dbs-restaurants.com/la-buvette, open Mon-Sat 8am-11pm, Sun 9am-11pm, pasta €13, Metro to Spagna, Tram 2 Flaminio

25 Here is where Antonio Canova, undoubtedly the best Italian neoclassicist sculptor, had his studio. His pupil Antonio Tadolini took over the studio, and his family owned it until well into the sixties. Today, you can have lunch or dinner or just a cup of coffee in the former **Canova Tadolini** studio among the many busts, statues, and plaster works.
Via del Babuino 150a, tel. 06-32110702, canovatadolini.com, open daily bar 7am-8pm, restaurant noon-midnight, €20, Metro to Spagna, Tram 2 Flaminio

28 **Babette** welcomes you with a basket of flavorful, crusty bread with homemade butter and a small soup as an appetizer at the French-Italian fusion restaurant. Enjoy an attractive courtyard garden and white linen tablecloths, along with the wonderful aroma of freshly baked bread and dishes that change seasonally.
Via Margutta 1d, tel. 06-3211559, babetteristorante.it, open Tue-Sat 9am-10:30pm, Sun 10am-10:30pm, €24, Metro to Flaminio, Tram 2 Flaminio

30 At **Buccone Vini e Olii** the many shelves are filled with wine, liqueur, and bottles of olive oil. Have a seat and order a glass and a few appetizers to start your evening.
Via di Ripetta 19/20, tel. 06-3612154, enotecabuccone.com, open Mon-Sat 10am-10pm, Sun 11am-10pm, glass wine €6, Metro to Flaminio, Tram 2 Flaminio

37 What began as a coffee roastery in 1922 by the Marziali family has now grown into a gourmet restaurant. For more than a hundred years, **Marziali 1922** has been the place to go for the finest coffees and, nowadays, for any meal of the day.
Via Po 80, tel. 06-43683859, marziali1922.com, open Mon-Sat 8am-11pm, €22, Tram 2, 19 Buenos Aires

SHOPPING

17 **Rinascente** is a well-known department store in Italy. The Tritone branch has eight floors dedicated to fine brands, luxury goods, and design. While browsing in the basement, you can admire an aqueduct from the time of Emperor Augustus.

Via del Tritone 61, rinascente.it, open Mon-Thu & Sun 10am-9pm, Fri & Sat 10am-10pm, Metro to Barberini, Tram 8 Venezia

22 Between Via del Corso and Via del Babuino is **Via Vittoria**—Rome's most perfumed street. Here you will find several ateliers that specialize in artisanal and exclusive fragrances. You can visit the luxury Italian atelier CULTI House or the American "lab" Le Labo.

Via Vittoria, Metro to Spagna, Tram 2 Flaminio

27 Small marble plaques with Roman sayings and Italian proverbs—it will be hard to find a more original souvenir. These signs are handmade in the store by the owner of **Il Marmoraro.** If you can't find a phrase you like, don't despair. You can place a custom order.

Via Margutta 53b, open Mon-Sat 9am-7pm, Metro to Spagna, Tram 2 Flaminio

29 If you are looking for an extremely sought-after sneaker or a classic one, there is only one place to go. At **Holypopstore,** they are passionate about the world of sneakers and streetwear. With a modern and minimalist interior, the store also just looks really cool.

Via del Vantaggio 46, holypopstore.com, open daily 11am-7pm, Metro to Flaminio, Tram 2 Flaminio

MORE TO EXPLORE

26 Once a center for marble studios, **Via Margutta** has been a magnet for artists for centuries, as evidenced by the Fontana degli Artisti. The popularity of the street exploded after the release of *Roman Holiday*. Filmmaker Fellini also

17

17

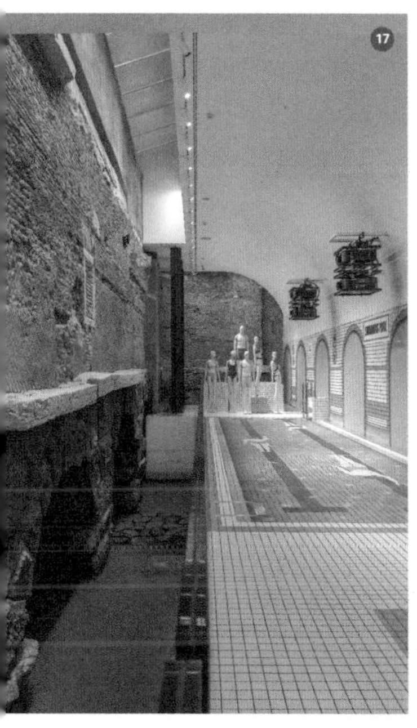

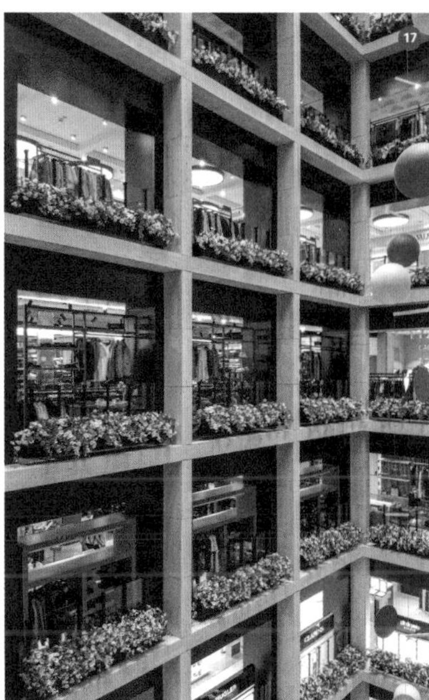

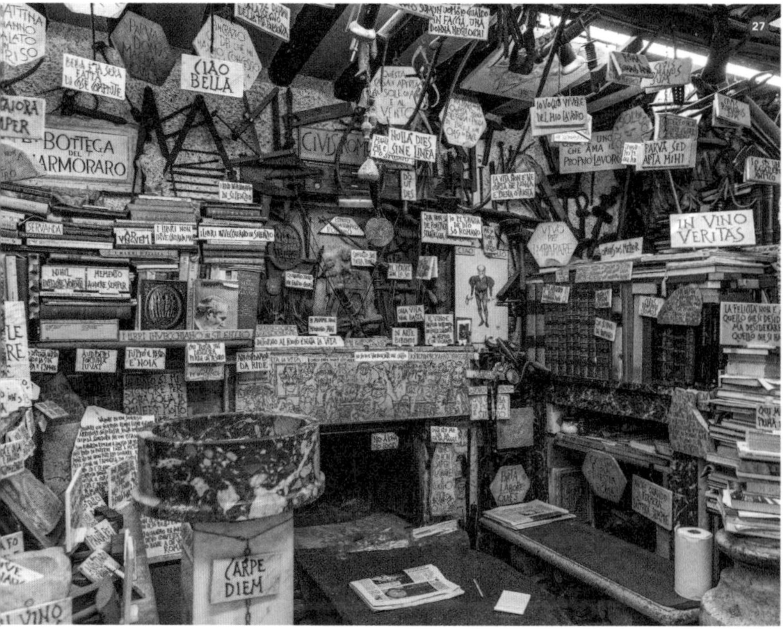
27
CIAO BELLA
BOTTEGA DEL MARMORARO
NULLA DIES SINE LINEA
IO VOGLIO VIVERE DEL MIO LAVORO
CHE AMA IL PROPRIO LAVORO
PARVA SED APTA MIHI
IN VINO VERITAS
CARPE DIEM

loved this quiet little street. Nowadays, few artists can afford to live here, but the street is still lined with galleries.

Via Margutta, Metro to Spagna, Tram 2 Flaminio

33 The **Giardino del Pincio** lies at the top of the Pincio Hill and serves as a starting point for exploring Villa Borghese. This estate was sold to the Pinci family after the Sack of Rome in the 5th century. The terrace offers spectacular views, especially at sunset.

Entrance Viale Gabriele d'Annunzio/Viale delle Magnolie, Metro to Flaminio, Tram 2 Flaminio

34 During the 17th century, the park surrounding **Villa Borghese** was the backyard of the influential cardinal Scipio Borghese. Now the expanse has high pine trees and a garden for all Romans. In addition to going for a walk, you can also enjoy cycling, picnicking, and rowing on the lake.

Entrance at Viale San Paolo del Brasile, open daily sunrise to sunset, free, Metro to Flaminio, Tram 2 Flaminio

35 In the beautiful, green, and yet slightly overwhelming surroundings of Villa Borghese, you will find a romantic, artificial lake with a small temple in the middle: **Tempo di Esculapio.** The temple was built in the late 18th century in neoclassical style by father and son Asprucci in honor of Aesculapius, god of medicine. Take a cute boat ride among turtles, geese, and ducks. Unfortunately, the temple itself cannot be visited.

Part of Villa Borghese, open daily sunrise to sunset, free, Metro to Flaminio Of Spagna, Tram 2 Flaminio

WALK 6

OSTIENSE, TESTACCIO & TRASTEVERE

ABOUT THE WALK

This walk takes you through three unique working-class neighborhoods. Ostiense is a former industrial area that has been given an artistic upgrade thanks to several large street-art festivals. Within the Aurelian walls is the 19th-century working-class neighborhood of Testaccio with many new restaurants and markets, and on the other side of the Tiber is the popular Trastevere—a cozy and vibrant area with a maze of small, charming streets and alleyways.

THE NEIGHBORHOODS

"Paint Over the Cracks" is a famous mural on Via dei Magazzini Generali, and it might be the best symbol for the transformation that **Ostiense** has undergone. The neighborhood is just south of the center and is seriously up-and-coming. Many great restaurants and bars have opened recently, and several large street-art festivals have given this once industrial neighborhood new life. The Gazometro (the giant iron cylinder where the gas supply for Rome used to be replenished daily) catches your eye everywhere, and the mural *Hunting Pollution* is iconic.

Testaccio is squeezed in between Via Marmorata and the Tiber River. This still quite distinctive Roman working-class neighborhood near the city center was literally and figuratively built around an old slaughterhouse, which is now a cultural hub filled with art galleries and restaurants. The neighborhood is named after Monte Testaccio—an ancient artificial mound/landfill that was created beginning in the 1st century from the discarded clay shards of olive oil containers. Today, Testaccio is a cozy yet lively district that does not (yet) attract many tourists: it is the only neighborhood in the center that still feels like a truly residential area.

Trastevere is the charming district on "the other side of the Tiber." In some parts of the neighborhood you can still see remnants of the medieval village that remained so long after the Middle Ages, and in other parts it's so busy, you almost have to walk over heads. There are not many authentic Trasteverini left, but the ones who are still here are proud of their neighborhood.

SHORT ON TIME? HERE ARE THE HIGHLIGHTS:

5 *HUNTING POLLUTION* + 6 PIRAMIDE DI CAIO CESTIO + 31 SANTA MARIA IN TRASTEVERE + 36 TEMPIETTO DEL BRAMANTE + 38 BELVEDERE DEL GIANICOLO

OSTIENSE, TESTACCIO & TRASTEVERE

1 Biffi/Bauhaus
2 Eataly
3 Romeow Cat Bistrot
4 Angelina Porto Fluviale
5 ***Hunting Pollution***
6 **Piramide di Caio Cestio**
7 Cimitero Acattolico
8 Emporio delle Spezie
9 Taverna Volpetti
10 Salumeria Volpetti
11 GetCool Testaccio
12 Più Bimbi
13 Osteria degli Amici
14 *Jumping Wolf*
15 Mattatoio di Roma
16 Mercato di Testaccio
17 Trapizzino
18 Porta Portese
19 Chiesa di San Francesco a Ripa
20 Santa Cecilia
21 Biscottificio Artigiano Innocenti
22 Ercoli 1928
23 Elvis Lives
24 Eggs
25 Aromaticus
26 Diciottomq
27 Sounds Familiar
28 Samovar
29 Bar San Calisto
30 Piazza di Santa Maria in Trastevere
31 **Santa Maria in Trastevere**
32 Calidarium
33 Chiesa di Santa Maria della Scala
34 Flake Design & Arredo
35 Santo
36 **Tempietto del Bramante**
37 Fontana dell'Acqua Paola
38 **Belvedere del Gianicolo/ Piazzale Giuseppe Garibaldi**

WALK 6 DESCRIPTION (approx. 6 mi/10 km)

Start with coffee 1 on Piazza Eugenio Biffi. Cross the street left to Circonvallazione Ostiense and turn right on Via Girolamo Benzoni for a food sensation 2. Return and bear right onto Via Pellegrino Matteucci. Turn left at Via Giacomo Bove 3. Walk right down the street, turn right again on Via Ostiense, and turn left across the intersection for something sweet 4. Walk down the street until you see the heron on the left corner 5. Turn right on Via delle Conce. At the traffic circle, turn on Viale del Campo Boari to reach the pyramid 6. Walk past the city gate to the cemetery on the left 7. Go back to Via Marmorata and walk left down the street and left again at the intersection 8. Take the first right and right again for Italian treats 9 10. Continue left on Via Marmorato and again take the first left 11. Turn left again for more stores 12 and then take the first right. Turn left on Via Zabaglia 13, then right on Via Galvani. When Monte Testaccio is on your left, look around for the mural 14. Continue on Via Galvani for industrial heritage 15 and the mercato on the right 16. Turn right on Via Aldo Manuzio, left on Via Lorenzo Ghiberti, and right on Via Giovanni Branca 17. Turn left at the end of the street to cross the bridge and visit the Sunday market 18. Continue down the street and turn right on Via Jacopa de' Settesoli in front of Saint Ludovica 19. From Via Anicia, turn onto Via della Madonna dell'Orto, and then turn left on Via di S. Michele 20. Take the first left. For the best cookies, take a right on Via delle Lucce 21. Walk back and take the next right for a unique restaurant 22. Walk back again and turn left on Viale di Trastevere. At the third intersection, turn right on Via di San Francesco a Ripa 23 and take the first street on the left 24 25. At the end of the street turn right 26. Take the first street right for vinyl 27. Walk across Piazza di San Calisto 28 29 and enter Piazza di Santa Maria in Trastevere for one of the oldest fountains 30 and churches in Rome 31. Walk around the church and immediately turn right for a classic souvenir 32. Walk back, take the next right and cross Piazza di Sant'Egidio. Keep left to Via della Scala, enter the church of the same name 33, and purchase handmade ceramics 34. Turn left on Via Garibaldi. Take the first street on the left, continue until the end, and turn right on Vicolo del Cedro. Turn left on Vicolo della Frusta 35. Follow the road to the church across the street 36 and meander up the hill. Pass the fountain 37 and take a right on Passeggiata del Gianicolo, ending at Piazzale Giuseppe Garibaldi 38.

SIGHTS & ATTRACTIONS

5 Rome is much more than antiquity, and this is immediately apparent in Ostiense—a former industrial area and now one of the city's most famous street art districts. Take, for example, the gigantic heron by artist Iena Cruz: ***Hunting Pollution*** is not only pretty, but also the largest mural in Europe made with 100 percent environmentally friendly paint that purifies the air to prevent pollution.
Via del Porto Fluviale, Metro B, B1 Piramide, Tram 8 Porta S. Paolo

6 When Egypt was part of the Roman Empire (and Julius Caesar courted Cleopatra), Rome went through a period of Egyptomania. Everything "Egypt" was hot, from obelisks to Egyptian gods. The nobleman Caio Cestio commissioned the building of **Piramide di Caio Cestio** and was buried here himself. When Emperor Aurelius built a new city wall more than two centuries later, the pyramid was incorporated into it. Currently, it can be viewed only from the outside.
Via Raffaele Persichetti, coopculture.it/it/poi/piramide-cestia, Metro B Piramide, Tram 8 Porta S. Paolo

7 Just along the Aurelian wall is the **Cimitero Acattolico,** a cemetery where all non-Catholic people who died in Rome were buried since the end of the 18th century. Many were foreigners, and some remarkably famous names are on the graves, such as John Keats, Percy Shelley, and Julius—Johann Wolfgang von Goethe's only son. The founder of the Italian communist party, Antonio Gramsci, is buried here as well.
Via Caio Cestio 6, cemeteryrome.it, open Mon-Sat 9am-4:30pm, Sun 9am-12:30pm, free (a contribution is requested), Metro B, B1 Piramide, Tram 8 Porta S. Paolo

14 Belgian street artist ROA's ***Jumping Wolf*** is nearly 100 feet (30 m) tall and has been Testaccio's icon since 2014. ROA has painted massive animal murals around the world. All his animals seem to have a delicate quality, as if they were pen drawings from a picture book. This wolf, of course, refers to the lupa from the city's founding legend.
Via Galvani 51F, Via Lorenzo Ghiberti, Metro B, B1 Piramide, Tram 8 Marmorata/Galvani

5

15 The **Mattatoio di Roma** is Rome's old slaughterhouse in Testaccio. It was built around 1890 by architect Gioacchino Ersoch and is a special and important industrial heritage site. In 2006 restorations of the complex started, and it's now a cultural center where you can see exhibitions and displays. The grounds are also worth exploring. Check out all the crazy corners for the most beautiful murals.
Piazza Orazio Giustiniani 4, mattatoioroma.it, open Tue-Sun 11am-8pm, free, Metro B, B1 Piramide, Tram 8 Marmorata/Galvani

19 You visit the **Chiesa di San Francesco a Ripa** mainly to admire Bernini's Saint Ludovica. She lies on her deathbed in the last chapel on the left. It's incredible how Bernini makes her robe undulate and move, suggesting there is a body hidden underneath.
Piazza di S. Francesco d'Assisi 88, sanfrancescoaripa.it, open daily 7:30am-12:30pm & 4-7:30pm, free, Tram 8 Trastevere

20 **Santa Cecilia** was built in the 9th century on the spot where, legend has it, the house of the holy Cecilia once stood. A devout Christian, she was

sentenced to death by being boiled in her own bath. For three days she sat in the hot tub, but nothing happened, so finally she was sent to be beheaded. After the executioner struck her three times on the neck with a sword, she still wouldn't die and ended up living another three days, singing during her entire ordeal. Today she is the patron saint of musicians.

Piazza di Santa Cecilia 22, benedettinesantacecilia.it, open Mon-Sat 10am-12:30pm & 4-6pm, free, Tram 8 Trastevere/Mastai

31 **Santa Maria in Trastevere,** dating to the 4th century, is one of the oldest churches in Rome. According to lore, in the year 38 CE a stream of oil flowed from the ground for an entire day, just to the right of the main altar. Afterward, this was interpreted as a sign of the imminent coming of Christ. The current building was constructed in the 12th century, and the gold-colored mosaics on the façade depict Mary and child. The church is built with materials that were stolen from the Baths of Caracalla. The columns date to antiquity.

Piazza di Santa Maria in Trastevere, santamariaintrastevere.it, open Mon-Fri 7:30am-8:30pm, Sat-Sun 7:30am-8pm, free, Tram 8 Belli

33 If you're into the Dutch masters, you'll want to visit the **Chiesa di Santa Maria della Scala.** In the first chapel on the right is a painting by Gerrit van Honthorst, who is better known in Rome as Gerardo delle Notti. As one of Utrecht's Caravaggists, he was a master at painting dramatic dark-light contrasts (chiaroscuro).

Piazza della Scala 23, open daily 10am-1pm & 4-7pm, free, Tram 8 Belli

36 Located in the courtyard of San Pietro in Montorio, **Tempietto del Bramante** is a tribute to harmony and symmetry. Bramante followed the teachings of Vitruvius and built the dimensions of the building to reflect the human scale. Commissioned by King Ferdinand and Queen Isabella of Spain to commemorate the apostle Peter, the small temple is said to stand exactly where Peter's crucifixion took place.

Piazza San Pietroin Montorio 2, sanpietroinmontorio.it, open Mon-Fri 8:30am-noon & 3-4pm, Sat-Sun 8:30am-noon, free, Tram 8 Trastevere/Mastai

37 **Fontana dell'Acqua Paola** plays a starring role in the opening scene of Paolo Sorrentino's movie *La Grande Bellezza*. The large fountain was the first mostra, or end of an aqueduct, on this side of the Tiber. Opposite the fountain is a beautiful view of the city. The three windows in the central arches once overlooked the botanical garden beyond.
Via Garibaldi, Tram 8 Trastevere/Mastai

FOOD & DRINK

1 Start your day at **Biffi,** an edgy and cozy restaurant with a wonderful menu and great terrace. They organize the "B2B"—back to brunch—on weekends, where they serve a fantastic club sandwich. Biffi's little brother is next door—the upscale restaurant **Bauhaus**—which is very stylish and intimate.
Piazza Eugenio Biffi 11, tel. 06-51435360, biffiroma.business.site, open daily 7:30-2am, €15, Metro B, B1 Garbatella

3 At **Romeow Cat Bistrot** cats have center stage. Owners Valentina and Maurizio wanted to open a place where people could enjoy a vegan breakfast, lunch, and dinner while also enjoying cats without having to own one themselves. It's not everyone's cup of tea, but it is a lot of fun.
Via Francesco Negri 15, tel. 06-57289203, romeowcatbistrot.com, open Tue-Sun 10am-12:30pm, 1-7:30pm & 8-11pm, €17, Metro B, B1 Piramide, Tram 8 Porta S. Paolo

4 The interior at **Angelina Porto Fluviale** is a stark contrast to the edgy murals surrounding it. It's located in a romantic, tastefully baroque cottage and is filled with candelabras, cute and decorative knickknacks, rustic furniture, and chandeliers. The fare is traditional Italian dishes with a modern twist, but mostly this is the place for specialty coffees, juices, and pastries.
Via del Porto Fluviale 5f, tel. 06-43688415, www.ristoranteangelina.it, open Mon-Fri 8-2am, Sat-Sun 9-2am, €16, Metro B, B1 Piramide, Tram 8 Porta S. Paolo

9 The brothers Volpetti have been "in love with good food" since 1973. That is the motto of their restaurant **Taverna Volpetti,** so it must be good. The antipasti

14

29

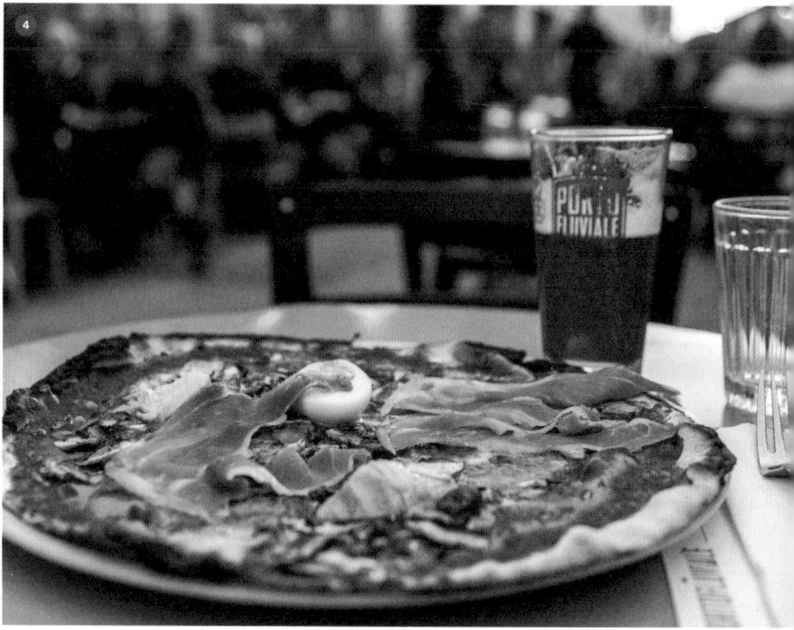
4
PORTO FLUVIALE

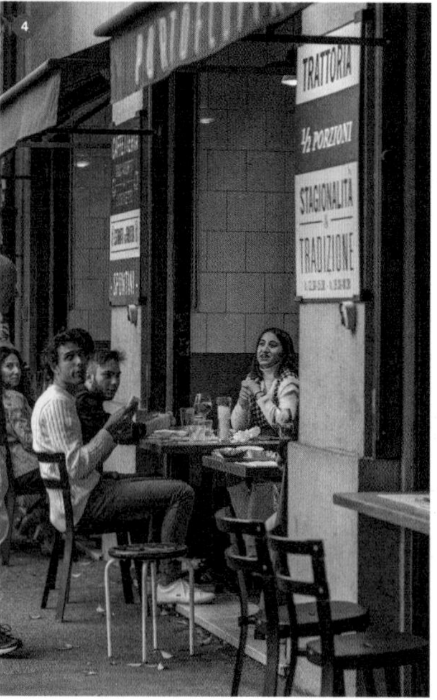

4
TRATTORIA
1/2 PORZIONI
STAGIONALITÀ E TRADIZIONE

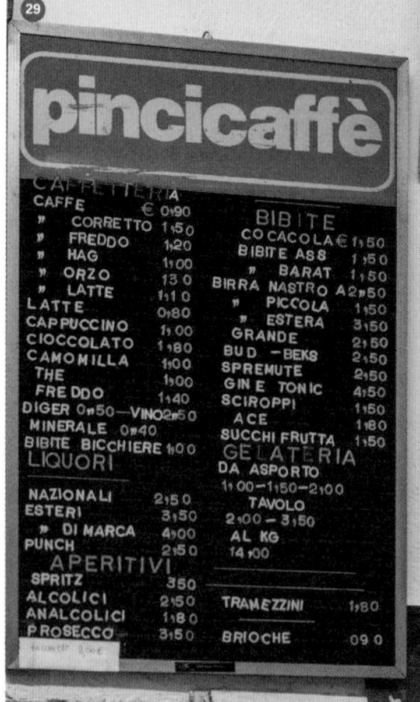

29
pincicaffè
CAFFETTERIA
CAFFE € 0,90
" CORRETTO 1,50
" FREDDO 1,20
" HAG 1,00
" ORZO 1,30
" LATTE 1,10
LATTE 0,80
CAPPUCCINO 1,00
CIOCCOLATO 1,80
CAMOMILLA 1,00
THE 1,00
FREDDO 1,40
DIGER 0,50—VINO 2,50
MINERALE 0,40
BIBITE BICCHIERE 1,00
LIQUORI
NAZIONALI 2,50
ESTERI 3,50
" DI MARCA 4,00
PUNCH 2,50
APERITIVI
SPRITZ 3,50
ALCOLICI 2,50
ANALCOLICI 1,80
PROSECCO 3,50
BIBITE
COCACOLA € 1,50
BIBITE ASS 1,50
" BARAT 1,50
BIRRA NASTRO A 2,50
" PICCOLA 1,50
" ESTERA 3,50
GRANDE 2,50
BUD - BEKS 2,50
SPREMUTE 2,50
GIN E TONIC 4,50
SCIROPPI 1,50
ACE 1,80
SUCCHI FRUTTA 1,50
GELATERIA
DA ASPORTO
1,00—1,50—2,00
TAVOLO
2,00 – 3,50
AL KG
14,00
TRAMEZZINI 1,80
BRIOCHE 0,90

combines cheeses and charcuterie from the family's own salumeria around the corner. Take one look at the menu, and you know you're in for a delicious meal.
Via Alessandro Volta 8, tel. 349-718-6894, tavernavolpetti.it, open Tue-Sat noon-3pm & 7-11pm, Sun noon-4:30pm, €26, Metro B, B1 Piramide, Tram 8 Marmorata/Galvani

13 This is not the place to come for a comfortable, trendy interior. **Osteria degli Amici** is rugged and modern with a few vintage details. The place bustles primarily because the food is exceptional. If you're craving traditional with a slight twist, reservations are recommended!
Via Galvani 18, tel. 06-5781466, osteriadegliamiciroma.it, open Mon & Wed-Sun 10am-midnight, pasta €12, Metro B, B1 Piramide, Tram 8 Marmorata/Galvani

17 Pizza meets tramezzino (a triangular sandwich) and becomes the **Trapizzino.** These Roman sandwiches are made from pizza dough and are filled with classic recipes such as polpetta (meatball) and parmigiana. It's a successful blend of traditional and street food, and it's practical as well.
Via Giovanni Branca 88, trapizzino.it, open Mon-Thu noon-midnight, Fri-Sat noon-1pm, Sun noon-midnight, trapizzino €5, Tram 8 Emporio

22 **Ercoli 1928** is a handsome and photogenic restaurant where a lot of time is spent preparing the flavors and presentation of all their dishes. For more than a hundred years people have been enjoying the traditional flavors of Italy and Spain. Many of the carefully selected ingredients can be purchased at the bottega dei sapori (flavor shop).
Via Zanazzo Giggi 4, tel. 06-96527412, ercoli1928.com, open daily 7:30-1am, €26, Tram 8 Trastevere/Mastai

24 The name of this restaurant is a give-away: at **Eggs** the egg plays the lead role in all dishes—recipes and presentation. If you choose gioco dell'ova (the egg game), you get six innovative bites served in an eggshell. The classic pasta carbonara is also recommended.
Via Natale del Grande 52, tel. 06-5817281, eggsroma.com, open daily noon-11pm, tasting €20, Tram 8 Trastevere

25 Bistro **Aromaticus** dishes up the yummiest salads, healthy bowls, and burgers with veggies and herbs straight from their own garden. You can have a seat in the window or on the terrace—the service is top notch, and the menu is versatile and prepared with passion. At Aromaticus they don't like labels like organic and vegetarian (although they would fit perfectly). They simply believe in good and healthy food.
Via Natale del Grande 6/7, tel. 06-88798381, aromaticus-roma.com, open Tue-Sun noon-11pm, €14, Tram 8 Trastevere

28 It's hard to choose among Trastevere's many restaurants and bars, but when in doubt, you can't go wrong with **Samovar.** Located on Piazza San Callisto, this small but exquisite bar is one of the places where the friendly staff makes you feel right at home. Order a coffee or a nice cold beer. There's live music on many Tuesday evenings, and there's always something entertaining outside on the square.
Piazza di S. Calisto 15, tel. 06-88799184, open Mon-Fri 6pm-2am, Sat-Sun noon-2am, pasta €10, Tram 8 Trastevere/Mastai

29 **Bar San Calisto** is a household name in Rome. During the day the terrace is the ideal place for a coffee, notably the caffè con panna—coffee with freshly whisked cream. At night you can have a drink and enjoy it on the square while listening to the live music.
Piazza di S. Calisto 3, tel. 06-5835869, open Mon-Sat 6-2am, Sun 7am-midnight, coffee €0.90, Tram 8 Trastevere/Mastai

35 **Santo** is off the beaten track and stands out due to the sturdy lights above the terrace and the urban jungle vibe. The interior is full of personality—robust and cozy. The dishes on the menu are based on Italian cuisine but always have an exciting twist. Every Wednesday there is live music, and on weekends around midnight the restaurant becomes a cocktail bar. Come here and you're guaranteed a great night out.
Via della Paglia 40, tel. 333-380-7008, santotrastevere.it, open Tue-Sat 6pm-2am, €24, Tram 8 Trastevere/Mastai

SHOPPING

❷ **Eataly** is a true sensation. A food emporium located in a former train station that is four stories high, it offers great local specialties in every corner—local cheeses, meats, dozens of types of pasta, wines sorted by region, preserves, chocolate, and much much more. Everything is from Italy. If you come here, be sure to have some extra room in your suitcase! There are also four restaurants where you can have lunch or dinner.

Piazzale 12 Ottobre 1492, eataly.it, open daily 9am-midnight, Metro B, B1 Piramide of Garbatella

❽ In this rather modest store the walls are lined with glass jars filled with just about every herb and spice imaginable. The jars are adorned with handwritten labels, and once you've found what you want, it's weighed on an antique scale. **Emporio delle Spezie** is a sensation.

Via Galvani 11, emporiodellespezie.it, open Mon-Sat 9am-1:30pm & 4-8pm, Metro B, B1 Piramide, Tram 8 Marmorata/Galvani

21

10 **Salumeria Volpetti** is run by two brothers, and since opening in 1973 they have filled their charming shop with Italian goodies. The offerings are huge, and the quality is amazing. There are local and certified meats, cheeses, pastries, and delicacies, and a wide selection of wines.

Via Marmorata 47, volpetti.com, open Mon 10am-3pm, Tue-Sat 10am-3pm & 5-9pm, Metro B, B1 Piramide, Tram 8 Marmorata/Galvani

11 A nice shop with friendly staff and a cool collection. **GetCool Testaccio** has beautiful, unique clothing items of good quality. The selection is always just a bit different from mainstream fashion.

Via Aldo Manuzio 14, open Mon-Sat 10am-2pm & 3:45-7:45pm, Metro B, B1 Piramide, Tram 8 Marmorata/Galvani

12 If you want to bring home a nice souvenir for the littlest people in your life, stop by **Più Bimbi,** which has two adjacent stores. One specializes in strollers, gadgets, and other baby gear, while the other focuses on cute baby clothes and accessories.

Via Luca della Robbia 34 & 36, open Mon 4-7:30pm, Tue-Sat 10am-7:30pm, Metro B, B1 Piramide, Tram 8 Marmorata/Galvani

21 The small and charming shop **Biscottificio Artigiano Innocenti,** a little outside the hustle and bustle of Trastevere, has wonderful cookies. There is a wide selection—bring some home as souvenirs, and help yourself to one, as well.

Via della Luce 21, open Mon-Sat 8am-7:30pm, Tram 8 Trastevere/Mastai

23 **Elvis Lives** brings a bit of rock 'n' roll to Trastevere. In addition to the headphones, the record players, and albums by the Beatles, the Ramones, and the Rollings Stones, you will find many vintage-inspired shirts with prints, Polaroid cameras, bags, and jewelry for those who want to combine rock and Rome.

Via di S. Francesco a Ripa 27, elvislives.scontrinoshop.com, open Mon-Sat 11am-2pm & 4-7pm, Tram 8 Trastevere

26 If you're looking for a cool vintage store, go to **Diciottomq.** The name of the shop describes its size: 18 square meters ("diciotto" means eighteen in Italian). It's filled with bomber jackets, leather coats, designer jeans, and other rad stuff. Quality is good, and the staff is friendly.

Piazza di S. Cosimato 51, open Mon-Sat 11am-8pm, Sun 3-8pm, Tram 8 Trastevere

27 Walk into this store to browse, and you are guaranteed to walk out the door with a retro vinyl record under your arm only an hour later. At **Sounds Familiar,** you can listen to various old records at your leisure but be sure to chat with one of the owners. They are all passionate music lovers and can talk to you about music for hours. Are you familiar with Italian disco?

Via di S. Francesco a Ripa 5, open Mon-Thu noon-8pm, Fri-Sun 11:30am-8:30pm, Tram 8 Trastevere

32 On a side street near Piazza di Santa Maria is a perfect place to find an old-fashioned, fun souvenir: paintings. An artist paints watercolors at the back of the gallery. His love for Rome is seen in his colorful and beautiful fountains, historic monuments, and characteristic streets. At **Calidarium** you are sure to find a little artwork of your favorite place in Rome.

Vicolo del Piede 18, open Mon-Sat noon-8pm, Sun noon-5pm, Tram 8 Belli

34 The cute shop **Flake Design & Arredo** in Trastevere sells only products made in Italy: traditional Deruta pottery, hand painted ceramics from Abruzzo, or colorful tableware from the Amalfi Coast. They can ship anything to any place in the world.

Via della Scala 45, shop.flakesarredo.com, open Mon-Sat 11am7pm, Tram 8 Belli

MORE TO EXPLORE

16 Not so long ago the **Mercato di Testaccio** was relocated with a totally new image as a result. Now, the market stalls are white "boxes," and vendors sell everything from fruits and vegetables to meats, pastries, flowers, and even

11

8
PAPRIKA
DOLCE
€5.00
PAPRIKA
FORTE
€5.00
PIMENTON
PEPE ROSA

30

clothing. Take your time to stroll past the different vendors and feel the vibe of this neighborhood.
Via Beniamino Franklin, open Mon-Sat 7am-3:30pm, Metro B, B1 Piramide, Tram 8 Marmorata/Galvani

18 In the 1940s, the black market at Campo de' Fiori was moved to Porta Portese. Today, the Sunday flea market **Porta Portese** is as popular as it's ever been. You can find anything here: furniture, lamps, paintings and figurines from almost any era, bedding, new and used clothes, vinyl, books, posters, historical newspapers, shirts of Roman soccer clubs, suitcases, shoes, watches, shells. The array of items seems endless.
Via Portuense (entrances at Piazza di Porta Portese and Piazza Ippolito Nicvo), open Sun 7am-2pm, Tram 8 Porta Portese

30 The **Piazza di Santa Maria in Trastevere** is the center of the Trastevere neighborhood. People are usually gathered around the fountain, which happens to be the oldest in Rome, dating to the 8th century. Of course, the fountain has been refurbished many times over the centuries; what you see now is a design by Renaissance architect Bramante. Bernini and Carlo Fontana added details later.
Piazza di Santa Maria in Trastevere, Tram 8 Belli

38 It's a good climb to reach the **Belvedere del Gianicolo** (Gianicolo Hill viewpoint), but there are many places to stop, and the view of the city is amazing. Nearby is the **Piazzale Giuseppe Garibaldi,** a monument to one of the most important figures in the struggle for the unification of Italy. The monument depicts several scenes from the risorgimento. Rome was the last city to be conquered in 1870, and the unification was complete. If you time it right, you can descend to Trastevere in time for a well-deserved aperitivo.
Piazzale Giuseppe Garibaldi, Tram 8 Trastevere/Mastai

WITH MORE TIME

The walks in this book will take you to most of the city's main highlights. Of course, there are still many sights worth seeing that are not included in these walks. These are listed below. Note that not all the sites listed are easily accessible by foot from the city center, but you can get to them all by using public transportation.

Ⓐ Located right in center of the Ostiense district, this former power plant was designed in the beginning of the 20th century by engineer Giovanni Montemartini and operated until the 1960s. **Centrale Montemartini** opened here in 1997 as temporary home for works from the Capitoline Museums as they were being renovated. The center was so successful that it became a permanent annex. The machines from the former plant provide a beautiful backdrop for the antique Roman sculptures. If you want to escape the crowds and still see world-class art, this is the place to go.
Via Ostiense 106, centralemontemartini.org, open Tue-Sun 9am-7pm, €7.50, Metro B, B1 Garbatella

Ⓑ **EUR** is short for Esposizione Universale di Roma. Mussolini commissioned this neighborhood, and construction began in the late 1930s and was completed in 1953. The Palazzo della Civiltà Italiana, known as the Square Colosseum, is an example of the way Mussolini personalized the architecture here. The number of arches, horizontal and vertical, are equal to the number of letters of his first and last name. Count them: six arches vertically for Benito and nine arches horizontally for Mussolini. At the bottom of the building are statues representing various professions. Today, the building is Fendi's headquarters. After admiring the palazzo, continue on to the mosaic fountains: Mosaici Della Fontana Monumentale Luminosa. It is a beautiful 1930s creation by three different artists. End your walk with coffee or at Caffè Palombini.
Quadrato della Concordia, palazzo does not open to the public, café daily 7am-9pm, lunch €14, Metro B, B1 Eur Magliana

Ⓒ **Villa Pamphilj** is Rome's largest urban park. Many locals come here to run, walk, bike—you name it. The park is also full of shady spots and beautiful Italian trees typical of the area. If you want to relax here with a weekend picnic, you can get a well-stocked basket (blanket included) from **ViVi Bistrot.** It also sells brunch, lunch, or coffee.

Via Aurelia Antica, Via Leone XIII, or Via Largo Casale Vigna Vecchia, vivi.it/store/villa-pamphili, open bistro Mar & Sep 8am-7pm, Apr-Aug 8am-7pm, Oct-Feb 8am-6pm, park free, bistro €15, Bus to Via Leone XIII/Villa Pamphili

Ⓓ The **Museo MAXXI** opened to the public in 2010 with a collection that provides an overview of 21st century Italian art in an international context. The impressive building was designed by top architect Zaha Hadid. Gigantic concrete elements seem to flow organically into each other—the space is as impressive as the works on display.

Via Guido Reni 4a, maxxi.art, open Tue-Sun 11am-7pm, €12, Tram 2 Flaminia/Reni

Ⓔ The very yellow interior of **Siciliainbocca al Flaminio**—with yellow walls, yellow chairs, and even yellow table linens—conjures Sicilian lemons and sunshine, and the menu takes you there. The restaurant offers a fresh fish-based menu.

Via Flaminia 390, siciliainboccaflaminio.com, open daily 11am-3pm & 7pm-midnight, €22, Tram 2 Tiziano

Ⓕ The history of the **Galleria Nazionale d'Arte Moderna e Contemporanea** (GNAM) is intertwined with the story of Italian unification, or the risorgimento. The museum was founded in 1883 to exhibit contemporary art from the unified Italy. The current building, a neoclassical palace, hails from 1911, designed by civil engineer and architect Cesare Bazzani for the International Art Exhibition that took place that year, which was also the 50th anniversary of Italian unification. It is an impressive building with an equally impressive art collection and a prime location next to Villa Borghese.

Via delle Belle Arti 131, lagallerianazionale.com, open Tue-Sun 9am-7pm, €11, Metro to Flaminio, Tram 3 Galleria Arte Moderna

Ⓖ At the turn of the 20th century, the capital of Italy moved from Florence to Rome. Subsequently, there was a building frenzy, and neighborhoods such as Prati (around 1910) and Garbatella (1920s) popped up. Architect Gino Coppedè was pretty much given a free pass when designing his **Quartiere Coppedè,** just east of Villa Borghese. Here he mixed the Liberty style with neo-Gothic, Greek, and Baroque influences, which resulted in a unique look. Nearby is the traditional bakery **Santi Sebastiano e Valentino.** Pull up a chair and enjoy fresh-baked bread, delicious pastries, and a full breakfast on weekends.

Quartiere Coppedè Piazza Mincio, bakery Via Tirso 107, open bakery Mon & Sun 7:30am-3pm, Tue-Sat 7:30am-11pm, lunch €15, Tram 2, 19 Buenos Aires

Ⓗ In contrast to the many historical monuments and museums, **Museo MACRO Testaccio** (Museum of Modern and Contemporary Art of Rome, Testaccio) is dedicated to modern art. Located in a former brewery that operated until 1971, the museum still sports the name, Società Birra Peroni Ghiaccia, on the side of its building. In the year 2000, architect Odile Decq won the competition to design a new 20th century wing, making the museum an interesting and effortless blend of industrial and modern architecture. The building alone is worth the visit—be sure to check out the cool toilets. After a visit, walk to the bustling Piazza Fiume for a good coffee at **Faro.**

Via Nizza 138, museomacro.it, open Tue-Fri noon-7pm, Sat-Sun 10am-7pm, free, Metro to Termini, Metro B Castro Pretorio

Ⓘ **Il Pigneto** (the pine forest) was once a site of villas and farmland, but around the beginning of the 20th century it was developed as a residential neighborhood and was inhabited by industrial workers and immigrants, later followed by bohemians, and then hipsters. Located about twenty minutes east the city center by Metro, you'll find narrow, cobblestoned streets, few tourists, fun bars, and lots of amazing street art. For lunch or dinner, head to Via del Pigneto where Borgo Pineto has a garden that's perfect for a picnic, a restaurant, and a gazebo for drinks.

Via Prenestina 216, borgopigneto.com, open Tue-Fri 7-11pm, Sat-Sun noon-3pm & 7-11pm, €18, Metro C Pigneto

Ⓙ **Via Appia Antica** was one of the most important streets in ancient Rome. You can still see palaces of ancient times, the first Christian catacombs, and graves of Roman nobility. It's very walkable and bikeable, and even though it's relatively close, you'll feel you've escaped the city. Be sure to visit the catacombs of San Calisto and San Sebastian and the tomb of Cecilia.
Via Appia Antica 136, Bus to Basilica S. Sebastiano

Ⓚ The town of Tivoli is a wonderful day trip outing. It is less than 25 miles (40 km) from Rome and is famous for the imperial country house **Villa d'Este** of Cardinal Ippolito II d'Este. This 16th century palazzo has a large showpiece garden with a wealth of fantastical fountains, monuments, and flowers. This country estate is a UNESCO World Heritage Site for a reason. Stop for lunch at **Ristorante Sibilla.** You will need to make reservations well in advance—the food and the view are amazing.
Piazza Trento 5, Tivoli, villadestetivoli.info, open palazzo Tue-Sun 8:45am-6:45pm, restaurant Tue-Sun 12:30pm-3pm & 7:30-10pm, palazzo €17, restaurant €20, train from Termini 4548 Tivoli

Ⓛ Another fun day trip is to the papal summer palace and gardens of **Castel Gandolfo.** It's located south of Rome in Castelli Romani Regional Park, which consists of villages near the volcanic lakes Albano and Nemi. The villages in the region have their own charm—Arricia is known for locally raised and Frascati for its wines. Visit Palazzo Pontificio, the Secret Garden, and the Vatican Observatory, and then have an Italian meal at **Ristorante Bucci,** with beautiful views of Lake Albano. A train leaves Termini station for Castel Gandolfo every hour.
Palazzo Pontificio: Piazza della Libertà, museivaticani.va, open Mon-Sat 8:30am-1pm, €17, Roma-Albano Train from Termini

Ⓜ **Fregene Beach** is one of the beaches closest to Rome, and it's the perfect place to cool down when the summer heat gets to you. There are a few fun beach bars where you can rent a chair and umbrella or enjoy fresh fish. Romans love to stay until the late afternoon, lingering over an Aperol spritz with toes buried in the sand. Singita Miracle Beach is a good choice for a sunset beach bar. Or make reservations at **La Baia,** one of the best fish restaurants in

Fregene. Even in the colder months you can have a great dinner here, followed by a walk along the shore. Fregene is about an hour's ride on the Cotral bus.
Via Silvi Marina, labaiadifregene.it, open Mon 9am-3pm, Tue-Sun 9am-10pm, €17, Termini FL5 Maccarese/Fregene and Bus 11 Viale Viareggio

(N) Board the train in Trastevere, and in forty minutes you'll arrive in Anguillara. Then, it's only a short taxi ride to **Lago di Bracciano** (Lake Bracciano), the ideal place for a relaxing day on the water. Romans love to leave their busy city behind and cool down at this lake in the crater of an inactive volcano.
Lago di Bracciano, turismobracciano.com, Train to Anguillara

INDEX

INDEX

SHOPPING

MORE TO EXPLORE

PRACTICAL INFORMATION

TRANSPORTATION

MOON
ROME WALKS
THIRD EDITION

AVALON TRAVEL
Hachette Book Group
555 12th Street, Suite 1850
Oakland, CA 94607, USA
www.moon.com

ISBN: 979-8-88647-090-1
Concept & Original Publication
"Time to Momo Rome"

time to momo

MO'MEDIA

Text and Walks
Maud Nolte

Translation
Cindi Heller

Design
Studio 100%, Oranje Vormgevers

Photography
Roy Bisschops
Marjolein den Hartog
Fiona Ruhe

Project Editor
Sophie Kreuze

AVALON TRAVEL

Project Editor
Lori Hobkirk

Typesetting
Timm Bryson

Cartography
Kat Bennett

Copy Editor
Lori Hobkirk

Proofreader
Susan Elderkin

Cover Design
Faceout Studio, Jeff Miller

Printed in China
by RR Donnelley
First US printing, November 2024

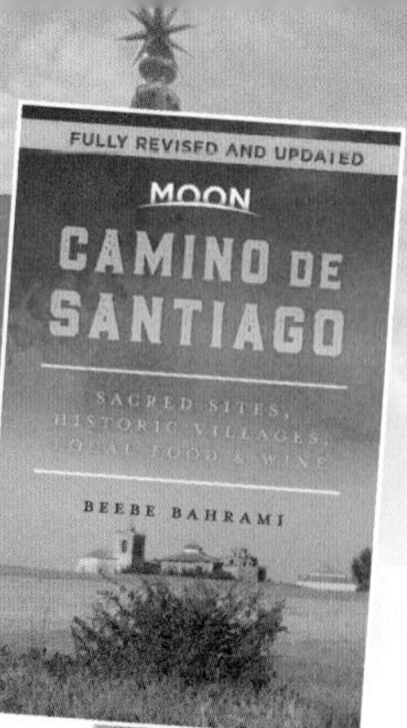
FULLY REVISED AND UPDATED
MOON
CAMINO DE SANTIAGO
SACRED SITES, HISTORIC VILLAGES, LOCAL FOOD & WINE
BEEBE BAHRAMI

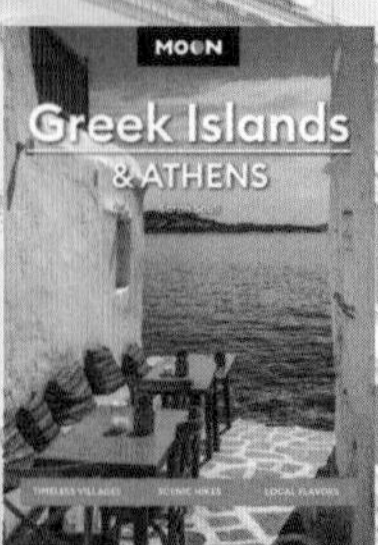
MOON
Greek Islands
& ATHENS

MOON
Azores

MOON
Provence &
the French Riviera

MOON
Amalfi Coas

MOON
IRELAND

MOON
NORMANDY
& BRITTANY
WITH MONT-SAINT MICHEL

MOON
BARCELONA
& MADRID
JESSICA JONES

MOON
Seville,
Granada & Andalusi
WITH CÓRDOBA, MÁLAGA, AND TANGIER

MOON
Norway

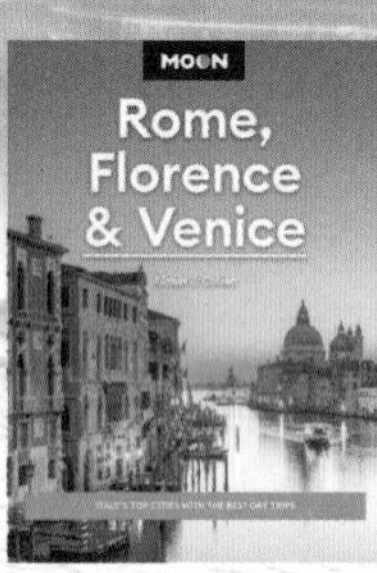
MOON
Rome,
Florence
& Venice

MOON
Morocco

MOON
EGYPT

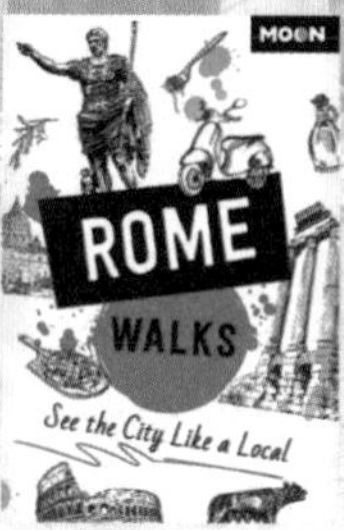